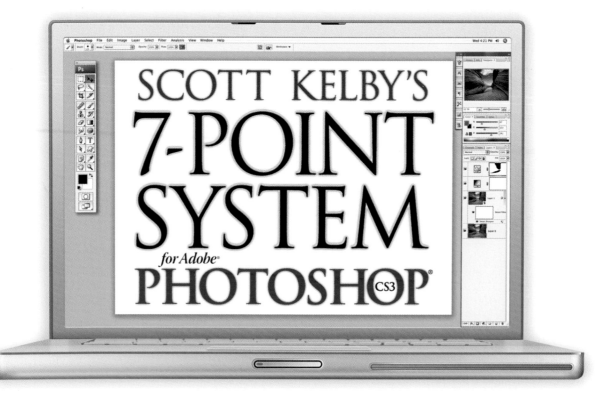

SCOTT KELBY'S
7-POINT
SYSTEM
for Adobe
PHOTOSHOP CS3

SCOTT KELBY'S 7-POINT SYSTEM
FOR ADOBE PHOTOSHOP CS3

The 7-Point System Book Team

CREATIVE DIRECTOR
Felix Nelson

TECHNICAL EDITORS
Kim Doty
Cindy Snyder

TRAFFIC DIRECTOR
Kim Gabriel

PRODUCTION MANAGER
Dave Damstra

DESIGNER
Jessica Maldonado

COVER DESIGN AND PHOTOGRAPHY
Scott Kelby

Published by
Peachpit Press

Copyright © 2008 by Peachpit Press

FIRST EDITION: October 2007

All rights reserved. No part of this book may be reproduced or transmitted in any form or by any means, electronic or mechanical, including photocopying, recording, or by any information storage and retrieval system, without written permission from the publisher, except for the inclusion of brief quotations in a review.

Composed in Myriad Pro and Trajan Pro by Kelby Media Group

Trademarks

All terms mentioned in this book that are known to be trademarks or service marks have been appropriately capitalized. Peachpit Press cannot attest to the accuracy of this information. Use of a term in this book should not be regarded as affecting the validity of any trademark or service mark.

Photoshop is a registered trademark of Adobe Systems, Inc.
Windows is a registered trademark of Microsoft Corp.

Warning and Disclaimer

This book is designed to provide information about Photoshop for digital photographers. Every effort has been made to make this book as complete and as accurate as possible, but no warranty of fitness is implied.

The information is provided on an as-is basis. The author and Peachpit Press shall have neither the liability nor responsibility to any person or entity with respect to any loss or damages arising from the information contained in this book or from the use of the discs or programs that may accompany it.

THIS PRODUCT IS NOT ENDORSED OR SPONSORED BY ADOBE SYSTEMS INCORPORATED, PUBLISHER OF ADOBE PHOTOSHOP CS3

ISBN 13: 978-0-321-50192-9
ISBN 10: 0-321-50192-6

9 8 7 6 5 4 3 2 1

www.kelbytraining.com

www.peachpit.com

For
my buddies:
Dave, Marvin, Mike,
Dave C., Matt, Corey,
RC, Roddy, Jeff R.,
Bill, Larry, Terry,
Felix, Tony, Scotty,
Jim, and Vanelli;

my family:
Jordan, Kira, and Jeff;

…and the love of my life,
Kalebra.

First, I want to thank my amazing wife Kalebra. We've been married 18 years, and just looking at her still makes my heart skip a beat, and again reminds me how much I adore her, how genuinely beautiful she is, and how I couldn't live without her. She's the type of woman love songs are written for, and I am, without a doubt, the luckiest man alive to have her as my wife.

Secondly, I want to thank my son Jordan, who spent many afternoons pulling me away from writing this book so we could play *Adventure Quest*. God has blessed our family with so many wonderful gifts, and I can see them all reflected in his eyes. I'm so proud of him, so thrilled to be his dad, and I dearly love watching him grow to be such a wonderful little guy, with such a tender and loving heart. (You're the greatest, little buddy.)

I also want to thank my baby daughter Kira for being such a little sweetie. My wife and I knew we were having a baby girl, we just didn't realize that she would in fact be "the cutest little baby in the whole wide world."

I also want to thank my brother Jeffrey for being such a positive influence in my life, for always taking the high road, for always knowing the right thing to say, and just the right time to say it, and for having so much of our dad in you. I'm honored to have you as my brother and my friend.

My heartfelt thanks go to the entire team at Kelby Media Group, who every day redefine what teamwork and dedication are all about. They are truly a special group of people, who come together to do some really amazing things (on really scary deadlines), and they do it with class, poise, and a can-do attitude that is truly inspiring. I'm so proud to be working with you all.

Thanks to my layout and production crew. In particular, I want to thank my friend and Creative Director Felix Nelson for his limitless talent, creativity, input, and just for his flat-out great ideas.

A heartfelt thanks goes to my Tech Editor Kim Doty, who did an amazing job in keeping this project on track and organized (while making sure I was organized, too, which is not easy to do). I am just so tickled to have you on our team, and working with you is really just a joy. Besides all your editing and management skills—you're going to make one really great mommy!

Also, a big, big thanks to Cindy Snyder, who helps test all the techniques in the book, and as always, she caught lots of little things that others would have missed.

My thanks to "The Michigan Layout Machine" Dave Damstra and Jessica Maldonado for giving the book such a tight, clean layout. We got truly lucky when we found you!

Thanks to my best buddy Dave Moser (Hey you!), who makes darn sure that everything we do is better than what we did. Thanks to Jean A. Kendra for her all support, and for keeping a lot of plates in the air while I'm writing these books. A very special thanks to my Executive Assistant Kathy Siler for all her hard work and dedication, and for keeping the rest of the business running like clockwork so I have time to work on books like this. I don't know what I'd do without you.

Thanks to my Publisher Nancy Ruenzel, and the incredibly dedicated team at Peachpit Press. You are very special people doing very special things, and it's a real honor to get to work with people who really just want to make great books. Also, many thanks to the awesome Ted "The L Shirt Connection" Waitt, Glenn Bisignani, and to marketing maverick Scott Cowlin.

Thanks to my friends at Adobe Systems, including Terry White, Kevin Connor, John Nack, Addy Roff, Cari Gushiken, Russell Brady, Mala Sharma, Julieanne Kost, John Loiacono, Tom Hogarty, Jennifer Stern, George Jardine, Dave Story, and Russell Preston Brown, and the amazing engineering team at Adobe (I don't know how you all do it). Gone but not forgotten: Barbara Rice, Rye Livingston, Bryan Lamkin, Deb Whitman, and Karen Gauthier.

Also thanks to my "Photoshop Guys" Dave Cross and Matt Kloskowski, for being such excellent sounding boards for the development of this book. You guys are the best! Also, thanks to Corey Barker (The Photoshop Lad) and to RC for coming on board and making my life easier and more fun.

I want to thank all the talented and gifted photographers who've taught me so much over the years, including: Bill Fortney, Moose Peterson, Joe McNally, Anne Cahill, Vincent Versace, David Ziser, Helene Glassman, and Jim DiVitale.

My personal thanks to Mike McCaskey for coming up with the idea for the "Refresher Course" lesson that wraps up this book.

Thanks to my mentors whose wisdom and whip-cracking have helped me immeasurably, including John Graden, Jack Lee, Dave Gales, Judy Farmer, and Douglas Poole.

Most importantly, I want to thank God, and His son Jesus Christ, for leading me to the woman of my dreams, for blessing us with two amazing children, for allowing me to make a living doing something I truly love, for always being there when I need Him, for blessing me with a wonderful, fulfilling, and happy life, and such a warm, loving family to share it with.

OTHER BOOKS BY SCOTT KELBY

Scott Kelby

Scott is Editor, Publisher, and co-founder of *Photoshop User* magazine, Editor-in-Chief of *Layers* magazine (the how-to magazine for everything Adobe), and is the host of the top-rated weekly video podcast *Photoshop User TV*.

He is President of the National Association of Photoshop Professionals (NAPP), the trade association for Adobe® Photoshop® users, and he's President of the software training, education, and publishing firm, Kelby Media Group, Inc.

Scott is a photographer, designer, and award-winning author of more than 40 books, including *The Photoshop CS3 Book for Digital Photographers, Photoshop Down & Dirty Tricks, The Lightroom Book for Digital Photographers, The Photoshop Channels Book, Photoshop Classic Effects, The iPhone Book, The iPod Book,* and *The Digital Photography Book.*

For three years straight, Scott has been honored with the distinction of being the world's #1 best-selling author of all computer and technology books, across all categories. His books have been translated into dozens of different languages, including Chinese, Russian, Spanish, Korean, Polish, Taiwanese, French, German, Italian, Japanese, Dutch, Swedish, Turkish, and Portuguese, among others, and he is a recipient of the prestigious Benjamin Franklin Award.

Scott is Training Director for the Adobe Photoshop Seminar Tour and Conference Technical Chair for the Photoshop World Conference & Expo. He's featured in a series of Adobe Photoshop training DVDs and has been training Adobe Photoshop users since 1993.

For more information on Scott, visit his daily blog at www.scottkelby.com.

TABLE OF CONTENTS www.kelbytraining.com

ADOBE CAMERA RAW PROCESSING

CURVES ADJUSTMENTS

SHADOW/HIGHLIGHT

PAINTING WITH LIGHT

CHANNELS ADJUSTMENTS

LAYER BLEND MODES & LAYER MASKS

SHARPENING TECHNIQUES

THE SEVEN POINTS ARE REVEALED RIGHT HERE!

How the 7-Point System Works:

Sorry for that *National Enquirer*-style headline up there, and I know you probably want to jump right over to Lesson 1 and start fixing photos, but if you do that (jump over there and skip this quick section where I reveal the seven points), you're going to wish you had read this (not now, but about halfway into Lesson 2, you're going to start saying things like, "Hey…" and "What the heck…?" and other stuff with three dots after it). But if you spend two minutes with me now, and let me explain the system so it makes sense, I promise you, you'll get much more out of the book. You'll totally "get" what we're trying to accomplish (and why I wrote it the way I did), and then the system will be a success for you.

I'll do this in a quick Q&A-style format, which is ideal for people with the attention span of a hamster. (Not you, mind you. Other people.) Here we go:

Q. So how is this 7- Point System going to help me?
A. Hey, first can we lose the attitude?

Q. Oh, sorry. It's been a really hectic day.
A. That's okay. Well, this book addresses what I've learned are the three biggest problems people have with editing their photos in Photoshop:

(1) They open a photo, and they know it looks bad, but they have no idea where to begin to fix it. They don't know what to fix first, what to fix next, or even how.

(2) If they already have a book on Photoshop (including one of mine), and they read about using something like Curves or Camera Raw, they can somewhat fix their photos while the book is open in front of them, but if they come back to Photoshop after their next shoot (which might be three days—or three weeks—later), they've pretty much forgotten what they learned three weeks ago, and now they're back to reading the book again, so things are moving really slowly, and that's very frustrating for them. What they learned doesn't "stick."

(3) They know Photoshop can fix their problem—they know it can not only make their photos look at least as good as it looked when they originally took the shot, it can make them look even better—they're just not sure which buttons and sliders will get them there.

Q. So this book is going to fix all three of those problems?
A. You betcha! We'll start with the first problem (they know it looks bad, but have no idea where to begin to fix it). You're going to do 21 lessons (they're like chapters, but they don't have chapter titles because they share a common theme, as you'll learn in a minute). Each lesson starts off with the original boring, flat, lifeless image as it came out of the camera. You download the exact same photos I used here in the book (even the RAW files), so you can follow right along with me every step of the way as I take you through the entire process—leaving nothing out—of going from flat to fantastic in just minutes.

Q. How is this different?

A. Well, think about it. Most Photoshop books show you how to do one thing per section, or one thing per chapter. For example, they might have a chapter on sharpening, or a chapter on Curves, or Levels, and they'll have you open a photo and perform, say, a Curves correction on a photo, and you're done. That's great, but here's the thing: as you've learned—that's not real life. You don't just open a photo, apply a quick single Curves adjustment, and then save the photo because it now looks amazing. In real life, that Curves adjustment only fixes one thing in a photo that needs 10 things fixed. Once again—you're stuck.

Hey, I'm not casting aspersions on other authors—my own books are guilty of this same thing, too. My best-selling book, *The Photoshop CS3 Book for Digital Photographers*, has a chapter on color correction, and it shows you step-by-step how to color correct a photo using Curves, and Levels, and Hue/Saturation, and a bunch of other color correction tools. But which one will fix the problem you have right now? Which do you use first? Second? Last? Which one is most effective? Which ones should you avoid? What's the proper order? See, there's something missing in the way we teach Photoshop—something that makes it stick. That's why I felt I had to write this book, and change the way we teach Photoshop.

Q. So this was all your idea?

A. Actually, it wasn't my idea—it was my brother Jeff's idea. I was showing him a slide show from a recent shoot, and there was one photo that really caught his eye. So I said, "Want to see the original?" and I popped open the original image in Photoshop, and his jaw just dropped. The original photo was this flat, lifeless, throwaway shot, but after my tweaks in Photoshop, the final image in my slide show looked pretty sweet (well, at least he thought so, but he is my brother after all, which in most cases would make him an easy audience, but he's a photographer, too, so he's pretty tough on my photography. And then there's that whole sibling rivalry thing, and well…I'm surprised he even sat through my slide show. Especially since Mom always liked him best. But I digress).

Anyway, he asked me if I'd show him how I did it, so he sat there and watched me take this dull, lifeless image through a series of steps that turned it into something that looked pretty darn good when I was done. Now, he's seen me use Photoshop for years, and he was still amazed, because although he uses Photoshop from time to time on his own images, he suffers from the same three problems I outlined earlier. Then he said something that made this book a reality. He said, "You need to write a book like that—a book where you start with a really crappy image [his words], and show people the exact steps, in order, you need to take to get it to there" (and he pointed to my screen, at the non-crappy finished photo that made his jaw drop earlier).

I told him, "I already do that in my books," but the more we talked about it, the more I realized that I really don't. Yes, all my stuff is step-by-step (that's what I always do), but I don't take it all the way from the raw, ugly original to final finished piece—every step of the way from start to finish. Instead, I would open a nicely corrected photo and show how to sharpen it. Or open a flat image, and show how to add contrast. Or a photo that was too red, and show how to remove the red—but not the whole thing—not the full monty of taking it from flat to fantastic. But I do now—in this book. Twenty-one times in a row. Twenty-one "crappy" photos to 21 finished pieces, and you're right there with me every step of the way—editing the images in Photoshop the same way I do in my own studio, on my own images.

Q. So, where did the seven points come in?
A. Well, about a year ago I started collecting "crappy" photos for this book (mostly my own, but some from friends who asked me to fix their photos), and I would do what it took (in Photoshop) to take them from boring to beautiful, and I'd record my steps along the way. It wasn't long before I realized that I was using the same adjustments, the same tools, and the same techniques over and over again. I also thought I wasn't using everything in Photoshop's arsenal, when in fact, I was using the same basic seven techniques again and again, no matter which image I was trying to fix. Just seven things. Not 70. Seven! Plus, for the most part I was using them in a particular order (with some small variance).

That's when I realized two things: (1) if I can distill this down to just these seven techniques, these "7 Points," then anybody would be able to learn this stuff (after all, learning everything about Photoshop is really daunting, but learning just seven things in Photoshop—that's a piece of cake!), and (2) if it's just seven things, I can have them repeat them again and again, so it finally, actually, really sticks. It's the repetition that's missing. That's why, when you come back two or three weeks later, you can't remember what to do first. ("Am I supposed to use Levels first? No, wait, did I change to Lab color first, then sharpen? No, wait, wasn't I supposed to create a new layer before I did that?") Does any of this sound familiar? If it does—this is the book for you, my friend. (By the way, even if it doesn't sound familiar—this is still the book for you. Just ask my publisher.) ;-)

Q. So I'm going to be doing the same thing over and over again?
A. Well, yeah. But that's the beauty of this book—you'll get really, really good at this stuff, because you'll do it over and over and over again. Luckily, each project is different—each image is different—but you still use the same seven adjustments in pretty much the same way, in pretty much in the same order. At some point, later in the book, you're going to go to do one of those seven points, and you're going to say to yourself, "Aw, this again? I already know this. I've done it a dozen times now." Bingo! That's it—that's the book at work. That's what it's all about. The whole idea is that you do this stuff again and again until it becomes second nature. You do it until my workflow becomes your workflow, and these seven points become just "stuff you already know how to do," so when you hear yourself say, "I already know this," you need to smile that I-already-know-this smile. You're "getting the system." The cool thing is—the system works. You're going to be a Photoshop shark in no time, because there's not a photo you're not going to be able to fix using this 7-Point System. Okay, technically, you might come across some crazy-crappy photo that it won't save, but you'll be able to kick the butt of almost any image you see (and certainly any image you shoot). (*Note:* I'm trademarking "crazy-crappy." It would make a great name for a band.)

Q. Okay, I get it. But can you please tell me the seven points before I burst an artery?
A. Okay, you've waited long enough. But before I tell you, just know this: you're not going to be blown away when I list them here (after all, they're all features already in Photoshop, probably ones you've used before. I'm not going to name some hidden feature that Adobe buried deep in the program that you have to unlock with a secret code). The secret to this system isn't the name of the techniques, it's how you use them, and that's what you learn through each lesson—putting this to work, in order, for you, and only using what you need to use. So, here are the seven points, starting with the first one:

① Adobe Camera Raw Processing

We always start by processing our photos (JPEGs, TIFFs, or RAW images) right within Photoshop's Adobe Camera Raw plug-in, as seen above, where we've opened a JPEG image there for editing (only Photoshop CS3 lets you open JPEGs and TIFFs in Camera Raw). This processing in Camera Raw is the key component of our 7-Point System for a number of reasons, including that editing the tone and color of your images using Camera Raw is much faster and dramatically easier than doing it in Photoshop itself, where it's much more complex, and significantly slower.

We're only going to concentrate on the most essential parts of Camera Raw in this process, so even though there are eight different panels within the Camera Raw interface (and a whole row of tools), we're only going to work in three of those panels, with only about 30% of Camera Raw's overall features—we don't need the rest for what we need to do, and that makes it even easier. So, to sum this first point up: Camera Raw has lots of bells of whistles and specialized features that you're not going to need to learn to master "The System."

ADOBE LIGHTROOM USERS: If you use Lightroom as part of your digital photography workflow, rather than using Camera Raw, you'll do the exact same steps I show in the book for Camera Raw, but you'll do them in Lightroom's Develop module instead. Lightroom's Develop module is based on Camera Raw, so by design it has the same sliders and functionality as Camera Raw, so don't let the black interface throw you—all the same sliders are there, in the same order. In the book, when I write, "Open your image in Camera Raw," instead you'll click on the photo in the Library module, jump over to the Develop module, and make your changes there.

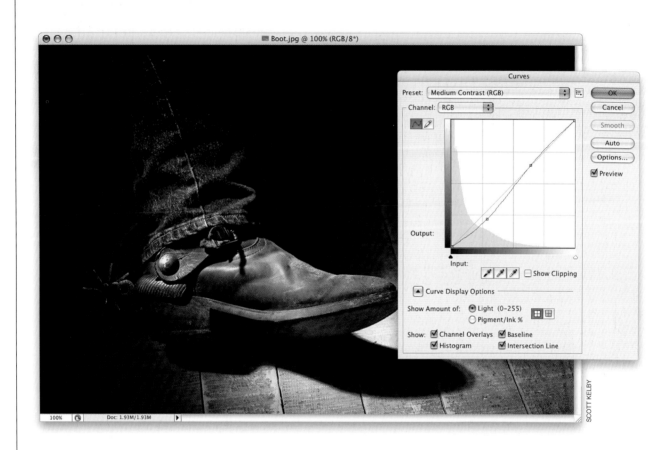

SCOTT KELBY

② Curves Adjustments

Since we create most of our contrast and do most of our color correction right in Camera Raw, we can get away with doing very little in Curves (where, without Camera Raw, you'd have to pretty much become a Curves expert, which for many people is a daunting task). But don't worry—even if you've never used Curves before, you'll be able to do the simple edits I'm going to show you in the book—the very first time. You don't need to become a pro at Curves, you just have to get good at the few things we'll be doing with Curves, and trust me, after 21 lessons of doing pretty much the same thing, you'll do it standing on your head.

SCOTT KELBY

3 Shadow/Highlight

Since we're going to pretty much eliminate highlight clipping problems back in Camera Raw (in the first point of the 7-Point System), if you have tonal problems in your photo after that, they're probably going to be in the shadow areas. That's where Photoshop's Shadow/Highlight control comes in, but we're going to use it in a more advanced way that gives you better results. Don't let that word "advanced" throw you—I didn't say, "We're going to use it in a complex or hard way." In fact, the method is really quite simple. It's just that we need better results than the default way of using this control will bring us, and as you get farther into the book, you'll see exactly why.

4 Painting with Light

The ability to control the light in your image gives you incredible control, but more than using this as a special effect (which is probably how most people think of "painting with light"), we're going to use it to fix exposure problems and bring out detail in areas that would have been lost otherwise.

This is one of the easiest, yet most powerful ways to get your photos looking like you wish they did, and once you do it a few times (putting light right where you want it, but in a much better way than simply dodging and burning), the light bulb is going to come on for you in a big way, and this alone will change the way you edit your images from here on out.

SCOTT KELBY

⑤ Channels Adjustments

This sounds like something that would be complicated, but it isn't. In fact, it's so simple that you'll be able to do it the very first time you try it, and every time thereafter, without breaking a sweat. We're using Lab color channels as a creative tool, and you're going to fall in love with this right off the bat, because basically it's going to show you three different versions of your photo (all three of which have more color vibrancy and color contrast), and all you have to do is choose the one you like best. It doesn't get much easier than that.

SCOTT KELBY

6 Layer Blend Modes & Layer Masks

You'll already know part of this technique because of the "painting with light" technique you'll have already learned. But, once again, this is one of those easy, yet surprisingly powerful, techniques that, when used the way I'll share in the book, becomes another key tool in your "I'm a Photoshop Shark" toolbox. What I like best about this part is it's really fun (and isn't fun the best thing to have?).

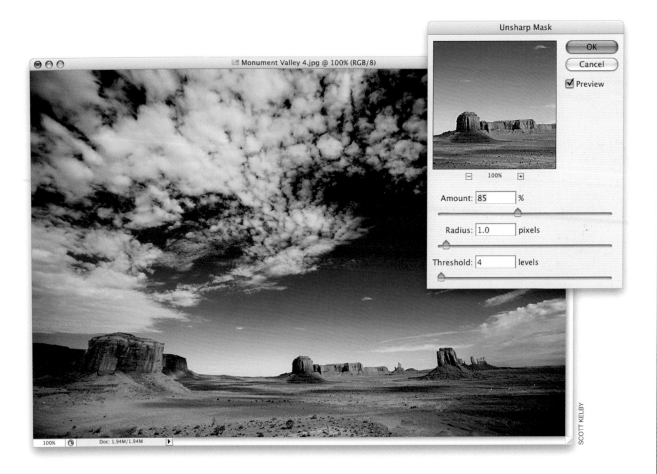

SCOTT KELBY

⑦ Sharpening Techniques

We sharpen every single image, usually twice: once at the very beginning, right within Camera Raw (which is called input sharpening), and once before we save the file (called output sharpening), where we sharpen based on whether you'll be sending your photo to the Web or if you're making a print (the amount is also based on the subject matter of your photo). We use Photoshop's Unsharp Mask filter for our sharpening, but then we add one extra little step that lets us apply more sharpening without damaging our photo. Besides which, you're going to learn how to add some one-click automation that lets you apply your sharpening like a pro by just pressing one button. Sweet!

So, those are the techniques that make up my 7-Point System, but don't let just the names of these techniques fool you, this is very powerful stuff. When it's applied the way I'm going to show you, in the order I'm going to show you, it comes together to give you a real plan—a real course of action that lets you know where to start, what to do next, and how to finish your photos so they look the way you want them to.

Q. So, will I use all seven points on every photo?
A. Nope. Thankfully, not every photo looks so bad that you'll need to apply all seven points every time. Most need at least four or five of the points, but don't worry—you'll get plenty of practice with all of them. Also, different photos use different points, so again—you'll get plenty of practice at determining which photos need what. Also, at the beginning of each lesson, in the top-left corner of the page, you'll see a list of which of the seven points are going to be used in that particular lesson, but even if you're already getting very comfortable with the seven points, you need to do every single lesson anyway.

Q. How come?
A. Along the way, I tossed in all kinds of other little tricks of the trade that aren't necessarily one of the seven points, but they made that particular photo look better, so if you do every lesson, you'll pick up more than just the 7-Point System—you'll learn some slick bonus tricks, as well.

Q. I love slick bonus tricks!
A. We all do. It's what separates us from the animals. That and satellite radio.

Q. So, do I have to start at Lesson 1?
A. Yeah, I'm afraid so. You need to start with Lesson 1, because in that lesson I have you create some sharpening actions that you not only use in each lesson, you'll use these in your own work after you're done with the book.

Q. So, is the book the same all the way through?
A. Actually, toward the end it starts to change as you start to change. By the time you get to last four or five lessons, you're going to know this stuff pretty darn well, so I stop spelling every little thing out, like I did in the earlier lessons. For example, in Lesson 6, when I need you to create a new layer, I might write an instruction like, "Create a new layer by clicking on the Create a New Layer icon at the bottom of the Layers panel—it's the second icon from the right." But in those last four or five lessons, I figure you've been around the block a bit, so I talk like I would to a colleague. At that point, when I need you to create a new layer, I just write, "Create a new layer," and that's it. I figure, if you don't know to create a new layer by the time you get to Lesson 18 or 19, you need to go back and start over—you're just not payin' attention (perhaps it's a drinking problem?).

Q. Is there anything the 7-Point System can't fix?
A. Absolutely. It can't fix bad photography. Here's what I mean: if you've got a good photo (it's reasonably sharp and well-composed), you can use The System to take this good photo and make it a great photo, but I can tell you this—it won't take a bad photo and make it a good photo. Believe me, I know. I've tried. The System just won't make a bad photo good. It'll make a decent photo better, a good photo great, and a great photo outrageous, but it can't fix bad composition, an out-of-focus

image, or a bad concept. You're always better off getting it right in the camera. That way, you can spend less time fixing it in Photoshop, and spend more time finishing it in Photoshop, which is infinitely more fun (and I've included many of my favorite finishing techniques right here in the book, so you'll pick those up, too).

Q. *What's the deal on the "Refresher Course" lesson at the end?*
A. A friend of mine came up with the idea, because sometimes he goes long periods of time between shoots (sometimes weeks, sometimes a month or more), and when he gets back, he said, since he's read the book once, he doesn't want to have to re-read the entire book again. He asked if I would include a quick refresher course that will quickly bring it all back. So, Chapter 21 is just that—a quick refresher course you can come back to if you take a long break from Photoshop (I call it "Mike's Refresher Course," but feel free to insert your own name). This refresher keeps you from having to relearn things you already learned when you first read the book. There's just enough info there to really jog your memory and get you back on track fast.

Q. *So where are the photos we can download?*
A. You can download the same photos I used in the book from the book's companion website at www.kelbytraining .com/7pointphotos. Of course, the whole idea is that once you're done with this book, you'll be applying my 7-Point System to your own photos, but for now, you should practice along with mine. See, I care.

Q. *Some of the original photos in the lessons look pretty, well…crappy (to quote your brother).*
A. Yeah, I know. Once I started putting the book together, I soon realized why other photographers hadn't done this original-photo-to-finished-product thing. It's because normally you only see a photographer's very best finished work— you don't see their misfires, or rejects, their "before" photos that would otherwise never see the light of day. But, to do a book like this, you have to let people see some of your crappy photos, too, and I can tell you from doing that here myself, it stinks (and that's not the word I wanted to use). But without these crappy originals, the book just wouldn't work, so I had to do it. (Of course, in retrospect, I could have just made up fake names for the photo credits beside each image, rather than identifying them as my own. I guess I should have thought of that before I sent the lessons to the publisher. Did I just say all that out loud?)

Q. *Any final tidbits or advice?*
A. Just remember that repetition is a key part of this program—there are literally hundreds of Photoshop books that teach you every single feature in the program, but this book isn't designed to do that. It's designed to teach you just the most important parts of just seven features, and have you apply them again and again and again, until they become second nature. Until they become your workflow. Until you become a Photoshop shark, which only happens when you're no longer scared of any photo. When you open a photo in Photoshop and right away know which adjustment to use, when to use it, which settings to use, and how to take your photos from flat to fabulous in no time.

I genuinely hope this book will give you a plan—a road map to follow—and help you finally get the results you've always wanted from your photography and Photoshop. My hope is that this learning methodology, with it's simplicity and repetition, will ultimately help you spend less time in front of Photoshop, and more time doing what you probably love best: taking photos and enjoying your final images or prints. Okay, now you can turn to Lesson 1 and dig right in.

LESSON 1

Before you kick into this lesson, make sure you read "The Seven Points are Revealed Right Here!" section right before this lesson (you'll need that before you go on). Now, this first lesson uses all seven points of the 7-Point System to help you get a feel for how this all works, but don't worry, not every photo in the book will require all seven (if most of your photos do require all seven, you probably have bigger problems than learning Photoshop. Hey, I'm only the messenger). This first shot was taken on a foggy beach in Los Osos, California.

Step One:
Open the unadjusted photo in Camera Raw (as shown here).

SCOTT KELBY

Step Two:

I always start by setting the white balance (the color of the light in your photo), and in this case, the photo is very gray. So, to warm it up, drag the Temperature slider to the right toward yellow (as shown here, where I dragged it to 7100).

Step Three:

Now let's brighten the highlights in the photo by dragging the Exposure slider to the right. In this case, the photo was very underexposed, so I dragged the slider until the Exposure read +1.30. You could drag even farther to the right without clipping the highlights (dragging so far that the brightest parts of the photo become pure white and lose all their detail). But at this point, the photo is already looking pretty washed out, so rather than relying on the histogram at the top right of the Camera Raw window, you have to rely on your eyes, and if you go much further, it looks pretty bad (go ahead and drag a little farther to the right and you'll see what I mean).

Step Four:

When a photo looks washed out, like this one, usually increasing the blacks (shadows) will bring back the saturation and density in the color enough to fix the image. So, drag the Blacks slider to the right until it looks good to you (I dragged over to 39 in the example shown here). We can keep adjusting sliders here in Camera Raw, but this is one of those cases where we're going to have to use Photoshop's Curves to really fix this problem, but you can see (if you compare the image here with the one in Step One) we've already made some progress. So, click the Open Image button at the bottom of the window to open the image in Photoshop.

Step Five:

Once the photo is open in Photoshop, click on the Create New Adjustment Layer icon at the bottom of the Layers panel and choose Curves from the pop-up menu. When the Curves dialog appears, there are a number of presets you can choose from in the pop-up menu at the top of the dialog. There are Curves effects presets (which we pretty much ignore in this book) and presets that create contrast. Go ahead and choose Strong Contrast (RGB) from the Preset menu, and you'll see it just gives us more of the same—it's brighter and more contrasty, but it doesn't look good. What we can do, though, is some simple Curves adjustments using the Curves Eyedroppers. That will do the trick.

Step Six:

In the Curves dialog, there are three Eyedropper tools beneath the curve grid (shadow, midtone, and highlight). Double-click on the shadow Eyedropper tool (it's the first one on the left—its icon is half-filled with black). This brings up the Select Target Shadow Color Picker (seen here). You're going to change the settings in the R, G, and B fields by simply typing in new numbers. Double-click in the R field to highlight it, type in a 7, then press the Tab key to jump to the G field. Enter 7 there, and then tab to the B field and type in 7 there, as well (so the R, G, and B fields all have the same setting of 7), then click OK. Having your shadow RGB values set at 7 works well for most color inkjet printing. If the shadows in your prints look a little too dark, then try 10, 10, and 10 instead.

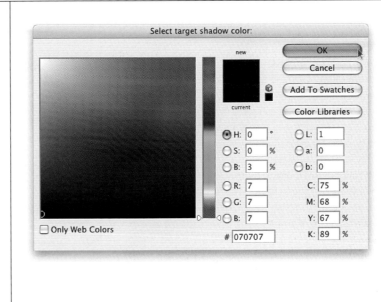

Step Seven:

Now double-click on the far-right Eyedropper (the highlight Eyedropper; the one half-filled with white). When the Select Target Highlight Color Picker appears, enter R: 245, G: 245, and B: 245. These numbers work well for holding the detail in highlights when you're printing to a color inkjet. Now click OK to lock in those new numbers. When it comes to setting the midtones (the center Eyedropper), you can leave the settings at their default setting of R: 128, G: 128, and B: 128, or if you like brighter midtones, you can use R: 133, G: 133, and B: 133. Personally, I use the 133 settings myself, and if you'd like to give that a try, double-click on the center midtone Eyedropper, enter those settings, then click OK.

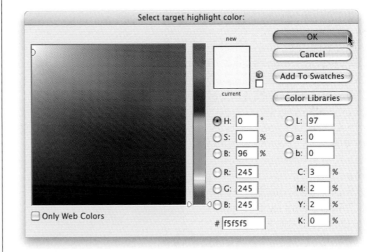

Step Eight:

Your Curves preferences are now set, and these new numbers will be in place from now on (unless you change them, reinstall Photoshop, replace your Preferences file, etc.). Now, let's put these new numbers to use. Click on the shadow Eyedropper and click on something in the photo that's supposed to be black. If you can't find something that's supposed to be black, just click on the darkest thing in the photo. In this case, it was pretty easy as it looks like the woman's riding pants are black, so click the Eyedropper once on her pants (as shown here) and now the shadow areas become neutral. You can see what a difference this one change made (and why we need to use Curves like this—rather than just using it to increase contrast).

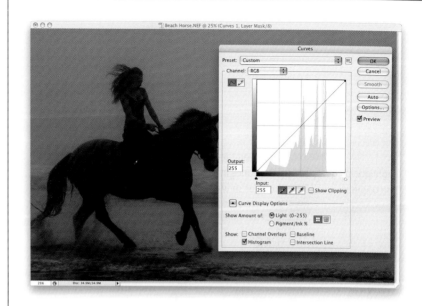

Step Nine:

Now, to set the highlights, you'll need to find something in the photo that's supposed to be white, and if you can't find anything white, then you should choose the brightest thing in the photo. Usually, this is fairly easy—you can just look and find something white—but this photo is still so drab and gray (and foggy), it's hard to determine what is the brightest part (and where to click the highlight Eyedropper). In this type of situation, Photoshop can show you the brightest part. Click OK in the Curves dialog and then choose Threshold from the Create New Adjustment Layer pop-up menu at the bottom of the Layers panel. When the Threshold dialog appears, drag the slider at the bottom of the dialog all the way to the right (which turns your screen black). Now drag it back to the left and the first area to appear in white is the brightest part.

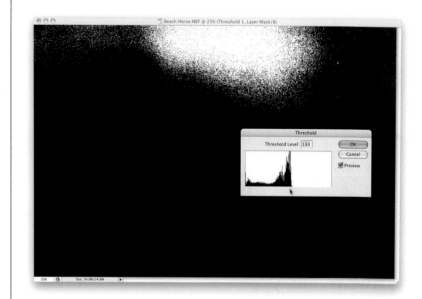

Step 10:

Now that you know where the brightest area is, just click OK to close the Threshold dialog, and then drag this adjustment layer into the Trash (at the bottom right of the Layers panel) to delete it. Double-click on the Curves adjustment layer thumbnail in your Layers panel to bring up the Curves dialog again. Click on the highlight Eyedropper, then click once in the brightest area of the photo (as shown here), and it makes your highlight areas neutral (also seen here). Click OK and then flatten these layers by clicking on the triangle in the top right of the Layers panel and choosing Flatten Image from the flyout menu.

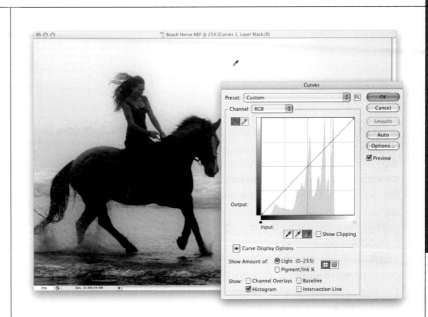

Step 11:

The horse and rider are backlit, so you're going to want to open up those darker areas, and bring out some detail in the horse using Photoshop's Shadow/Highlight controls. We're going to apply the Shadow/Highlight adjustment as if it was an adjustment layer (with a layer mask of its own) by pulling a little CS3 trick: we apply it as a Smart Filters layer, so it acts like an adjustment layer. You start by clicking on the Background layer in the Layers panel, then pressing Command-J (PC: Ctrl-J) to duplicate it. Then go under the Filter menu and choose Convert for Smart Filters (as shown here). In the resulting warning dialog, click OK.

Step 12:

Now go under the Image menu, under Adjustments, and choose Shadow/Highlight (it's one of only two choices in this menu that aren't grayed out). The default setting for this dialog is to open up your shadows by 50%, and I find that in most cases that's way too much (as in this case). So drag the Shadows Amount slider back to the left until it reads only 16% (as shown here), and click OK. This brightens all the shadow areas in the entire photo by 16%, but we only want the shadows affected that are on the horse and rider. In the next step, we'll be able to do just that thanks to our little CS3 Smart Filters layer trick.

Step 13:

Go to the Layers panel, and you'll see that a layer mask for the Shadow/Highlight adjustment has been added below your duplicate layer. The layer mask is white, meaning you see the full effect of your Shadow/Highlight adjustment over your entire image. To change that, click on the layer mask thumbnail to select it, and then press Command-I (PC: Ctrl-I) to Invert the thumbnail to black, hiding your Shadow/Highlight adjustment from view. Now, press D to set your Foreground color to white and press B to get the Brush tool. Click on the brush thumbnail in the Options Bar, and choose a medium-sized, soft-edged brush from the Brush Picker. Paint over the horse and rider, and now just those areas get their shadows opened up by 16% (as you paint, it reveals the Shadow/Highlight adjustment). Then, from the Layers panel's flyout menu, choose Flatten Image to flatten your layers.

Step 14:

Now, if you step back and look at the photo in Step 13, you'll see that the top one-third of the photo looks lighter than the rest of the photo. To balance out the top one-third of the photo, we're going to use a trick that is used to darken skies (which actually gives us the effect of adding a neutral density gradient filter over the camera's lens). Press D to set your Foreground color to black, and then choose Gradient from the Create New Adjustment Layer pop-up menu at the bottom of the Layers panel. When the dialog appears, it puts the dark part of the gradient at the bottom of the image (and we need it at the top), so turn on the Reverse checkbox (as shown here).

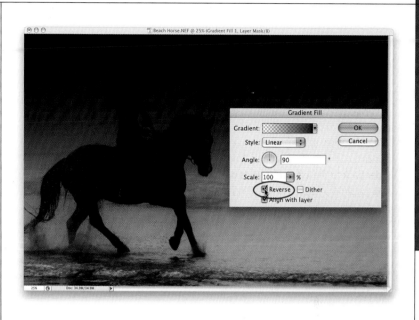

Step 15:

By default, the gradient covers the full range of your photo (from top to bottom), but you can control how far down the gradient extends by clicking on the gradient thumbnail in the dialog, which brings up the Gradient Editor. You'll see a large horizontal gradient ramp towards the bottom of the dialog. Click on the top-right opacity stop (the one filled with white), and drag it to the left. After you drag a little bit, release the mouse button and you'll see how your gradient is moving upward. Drag just past the center of the gradient (as shown here) and then click OK in the Editor and Gradient Fill dialogs.

Step 16:

To blend your gradient in with the photo (so it's just not a black-to-transparent gradient), in the Layers panel, change the blend mode of this layer to Soft Light. This blends the gradient with the rest of your photo, and in this case, balances the top one-third of the photo with the bottom two-thirds. Compare the photo now with the one shown in Step 13, where the top one-third is a little too bright. Again, choose Flatten Image from the Layers panel's flyout menu to flatten the layers.

Note: You'll do this same exact technique throughout the book, but usually on landscape photos to darken the top of the sky, and then have it gradually blend into the rest of the photo.

Step 17:

Although we warmed the white balance a little bit back in Camera Raw when we started, the photo still looks fairly gray. To warm it up even more, we can add what is the Photoshop equivalent of a traditional warming filter—Photoshop's Photo Filter. Click on the Layers panel's Create New Adjustment Layer icon and choose Photo Filter. When the Photo Filter dialog appears (shown here), leave the Filter set to its default, Warming Filter (85), but increase the Density to 40% (think of the Density slider as an Amount slider), click OK, and flatten your layers.

Step 18:

Now we're going to use one of my favorite techniques for punching up the color—a Lab color move (this is a simplified version of a technique I learned from the father of Photoshop color, Dan Margulis). You start by going under the Image menu, under Mode, and choosing Lab Color (as shown here). When you convert to Lab color (which is a totally non-destructive move, by the way), your image looks the same, but it's no longer made up of a Red channel, a Green channel, and a Blue channel (like RGB color). In Lab color, your image is made up of a Lightness channel (where all the detail is), an "a" channel (with half the color), and a "b" channel (with the rest of the color).

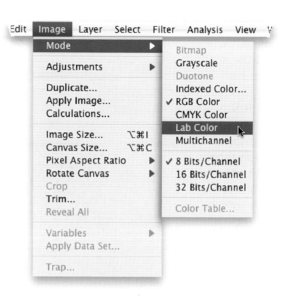

Step 19:

Now that you're in Lab color, go under the Image menu and choose Apply Image (this lets you apply a channel to your image using the same blend modes you have when using layers). When the Apply Image dialog appears (shown here), choose Soft Light from the Blending pop-up menu. Now, you get to choose one of three channels (the Lab composite channel, the "a" channel, or the "b" channel). Each gives a different color and contrast look to your photo, and you can try out each look by choosing them from the Channel pop-up menu. The default channel is the Lab channel, and its look is shown here. It doesn't look bad, but it doesn't look great.

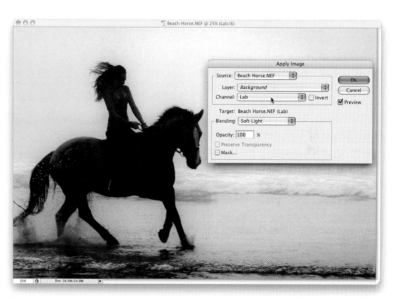

Step 20:

Now go ahead and try choosing the "a" channel, then the "b" channel. In this case, the "b" channel looks best to me (this is totally a creative choice, so you have to choose which looks best to you, but just for the sake of this particular project, choose "b." If you think this is a little too intense, you can also reduce the Opacity setting, which you can see in the next step I did). Now click OK to apply your changes. Compare the image here with the image in Step 17, and you can see how much warmer, richer, and more colorful the image looks here. Before we go on, go back to the Image menu, under Mode, and change your photo back to RGB color.

Step 21:

Now it's time to sharpen the image. We always try to do this as the last thing we do before saving the file (we can sharpen once in Camera Raw, which you'll learn a little later in the book, and then do one final sharpening before we save here in Photoshop, which we generally call "sharpening for print"). Since you're going to be sharpening as just about the last thing you do to every single photo you edit in this book, you might as well make your life easier by creating some actions that will do the work for you. So, go to the Actions panel (choose Actions from the Window menu), click on the Create New Action icon at the bottom of the panel, and when the New Action dialog appears, name your action Sharpen Medium. Choose an F-key to assign this sharpening to (so you can apply this sharpening anytime by just pressing this key). Now click the Record button.

Step 22:

Go under the Filter menu, under Sharpen, and choose Unsharp Mask. When the Unsharp Mask dialog appears, we'll apply a medium amount of sharpening, so set the Amount to 85%, the Radius to 1.0, and the Threshold to 4. Then click OK.

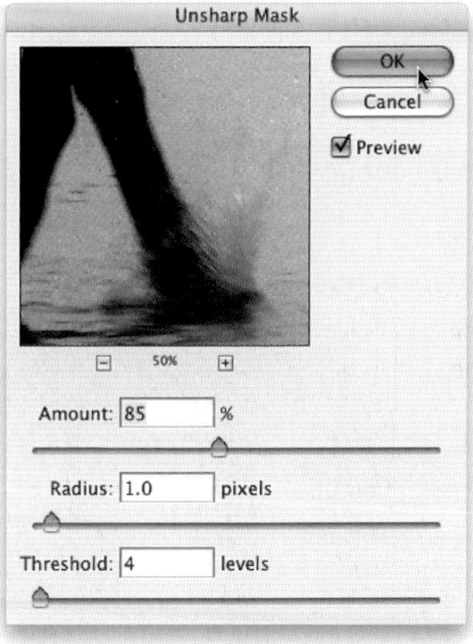

Unsharp Mask

OK

Cancel

☑ Preview

⊟ 50% ⊞

Amount: 85 %

Radius: 1.0 pixels

Threshold: 4 levels

Step 23:

Applying sharpening directly to a color photo can sometimes cause color halos, color artifacts, or other color problems. So, immediately after you click OK in the Unsharp Mask dialog, go under the Edit menu and choose Fade Unsharp Mask. This brings up the Fade dialog, where you'll choose Luminosity from the Mode pop-up menu (as shown here) and click OK. What this does is applies the sharpening to the luminosity (detail) of the photo, and avoids the color channels, and the problems that sharpening the color channels causes. You'll basically do this every time you apply the Unsharp Mask filter to a color photo, which is all the more reason why you want an action to do all this for you with the push of just one button. Speaking of buttons—head over to the Actions panel, and click on the Stop Playing/Recording icon (it's the first icon from the left).

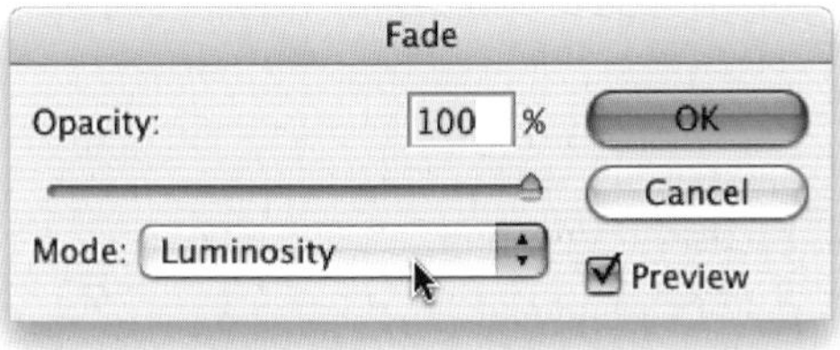

Fade

Opacity: 100 %

OK

Cancel

Mode: Luminosity

☑ Preview

Step 24:

If you look in the Actions panel, you'll see your new action (the one you named "Sharpen Medium"), and under it a list of what running that action will apply (the Unsharp Mask filter, and then the Fade command). When you create an action, it remembers all the settings you entered in the dialogs as well, so when you apply it, it will apply the exact settings you recorded (just click on the right-facing triangle to the left of the action step to see the exact settings).

Step 25:

While we're recording actions, let's go ahead and record two more (this will save you loads of time later). One will be a real punchy, tight sharpening for images with lots of well-defined edges (like buildings, cars, architectural elements, anything with lots of metal, etc.), and the other will be a low sharpening action (for images where the subject is softer in nature, like people, flowers, animals, etc.). Start by going ahead and saving your current document (go under the File menu and choose Save, as shown here), because if we apply two more passes of sharpening to this photo, it's pretty much going to trash it.

Step 26:
Now go back to the Actions panel, click on the Create New Action icon, and name this one "Sharpen High" (as shown here). Then choose a different F-key for this action, and click the Record button.

Step 27:
Bring up the Unsharp Mask dialog again (go under the Filter menu, under Sharpen, and choose Unsharp Mask), but this time for Amount enter 120%, for Radius enter 1.0, and for Threshold enter 3, then click OK. Now go under the Edit menu and choose Fade Unsharp Mask, change the Mode to Luminosity, and click OK. Then go back to the Actions panel and click on the Stop Playing/Recording icon. That's two down, one to go.

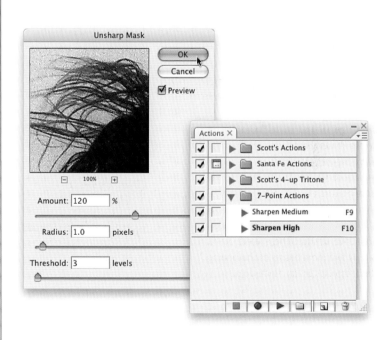

Step 28:

Again, in the Actions panel, click on the Create New Action icon, and name this one "Sharpen Low" (as shown here). Choose a different F-key for this action, and click the Record button.

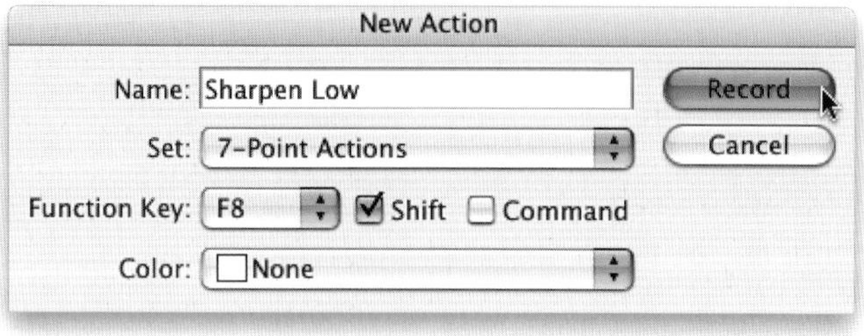

New Action

Name: Sharpen Low

Set: 7-Point Actions

Function Key: F8 ☑ Shift ☐ Command

Color: ☐ None

Record

Cancel

Step 29:

Now bring up the Unsharp Mask dialog again. For Amount enter 100%, for Radius enter 1.0, for Threshold enter 10 (as shown here), and click OK. Next, go to the Edit menu, choose Fade Unsharp Mask, and change the Mode to Luminosity. Click OK, then go to the Actions panel and click on the Stop Playing/Recording icon.

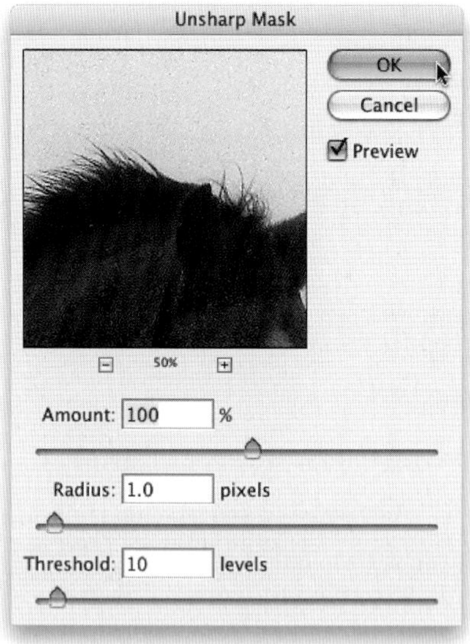

Unsharp Mask

OK

Cancel

☑ Preview

50%

Amount: 100 %

Radius: 1.0 pixels

Threshold: 10 levels

Step 30:

When you look in the Actions panel, you'll have three different actions (as seen here), and you can drag them into the same order you see here by simply clicking-and-dragging them into the order you want (just like you rearrange the order of layers in the Layers panel). Now, go under the File menu and choose Revert, which reverts your photo back to how it looked when you last saved it (which was right before the last two sharpenings). The before and after images are shown below.

Before

After

LESSON 2

Shot at the Marin Headlands, just across the Golden Gate Bridge, this shot looks like it was set up, but it wasn't (we drove up and the car was just like you see it). The light on the car looked fairly nice, but the car was backlit, so the side facing the camera is too dark, and the sky is brighter than it was at sunset. You're going to use most (but not all) of the 7-Point System to bring this photo back to life, but what really makes this work is a double-processing trick in Camera Raw using Smart Objects. Don't worry—it's easier than it sounds.

Step One:

Here's the original, unadjusted RAW shot as it was taken. When you open a photo shot in your camera's RAW mode, it opens in Adobe Photoshop's Camera Raw window (as shown here). *Note:* If you opened this photo from Adobe Bridge CS3, it opens in the same Camera Raw window, but it opens in Bridge's version of Camera Raw instead.

SCOTT KELBY

Step Two:

We'll start in the Basic panel by adjusting the white balance (I've zoomed in a little here so the controls are easier to see). In this case, we're not trying to find the proper daylight white balance, instead we're using the White Balance controls as a creative tool to make the sunset look warmer and more like sunrise. So, click-and-drag the Temperature slider to the left until it reads 5000, which makes the photo look more yellow and warmer (like sunset). Then click-and-drag the Tint slider directly below it to the right (towards magenta) until it reads around +18, which makes the overall color a bit more purple, and more like sunrise (as seen here).

Step Three:

In this photo, the sun is just setting and the area around the sun is very bright and blown out. If you look at the histogram in the Camera Raw window in the previous step, you can see that in the top-right corner of the histogram, there is a solid white triangle. That's warning you that part of the detail in the photo has been clipped (meaning, it's so bright in those areas, there's no detail there at all). To bring back as much of that detail as possible, first drag the Exposure slider to the left a bit, and then drag the Recovery slider to the right (as shown here) until the warning triangle turns black, indicating that you've recovered those lost highlights. If you compare the photo here with the one in the previous step, you can see how the area around the sun and clouds is now much darker and more defined.

Step Four:

At this point, we've made the changes we need to this photo (which, when you think about it, are pretty minor—we just changed the overall mood of the photo to a warmer sunrise color, and we darkened the sky a bit by recovering some of the clipped highlights). Now we're going to open the photo in Photoshop, but don't just click the Open Image button. Instead, press-and-hold the Shift key first, and you'll see the Open Image button change into the Open Object button (as shown here). Now this photo will open in Photoshop as a Smart Object (you'll see why this is so important—and really cool—in just a minute or two, but for now just press-and-hold the Shift key and click Open Object).

Step Five:

When the photo opens in Photoshop, the way you can tell the image was imported as a Smart Object is to go to the Layers panel and look in the bottom-right corner of the image's layer thumbnail. If you see a little curled page icon in that bottom-right corner (as you do here), then it's a Smart Object. If you don't see that little icon, it means you forgot to press-and-hold the Shift key in the last step. So, if you don't see that icon, pause for just a moment to really marinate in the embarrassment, then reopen the photo in Camera Raw (all the changes you made will still be in place), press-and-hold the Shift key, and click Open Object. Now look for that little icon in the Layers panel. If it's still not there, I'm not entirely sure you should be using Photoshop at all. (I'm just kidding. Kinda.)

Step Six:

Now we need a copy of that layer, but if we just click-and-drag that Smart Object layer down to the Create a New Layer icon (which creates a copy of your dragged layer), it automatically links the two image layers together. So any color adjustments you make to one layer are also made to the other layer. Sometimes that's exactly what you want, but in this case, we need to be able to adjust the look of each layer individually. So, to copy the layer, but break that adjust-one-of-us/adjust-both-of-us link, just Control-click (PC: Right-click) to the right of the layer's name and a contextual menu will appear. Choose New Smart Object via Copy from that menu.

Step Seven:

Now you have two Smart Object layers; they're identical, but you can now adjust them independently of each other. Reopen this copied layer in Camera Raw by double-clicking directly on the layer's thumbnail (as shown here).

Step Eight:

In the original photo, after we used the Recovery slider, the sky looked pretty good, but the car was still way too dark. So, now we'll get the exposure on the car looking good without any regard for how the sky looks, because we have a version of the exact same photo with a good sky waiting for us back in Photoshop. So, in the Basic panel, drag the Exposure slider to the right to +1.45 to brighten up the whole scene (as you do this, you can see the sky totally blow out and turn almost white. Don't let that throw you, though— press on!). Now, lower the Recovery slider back down to 0 to bring back as many highlights as possible on the car itself. Then increase the Fill Light amount to 13, which opens up the shadow areas and lets you see more detail in the dark areas of the car (as you can see here).

Step Nine:

Once you've got the car looking good, just click OK, and in Photoshop your layer is automatically updated with your new changes. Now, if you look in the Layers panel, you should see two layers—the top layer being the one with the nicely exposed car, and a bottom layer with a nicely exposed sky. So, the elements you need are all here: a perfect sky and a well-lit car. Now you have to "paint with light" to combine the two photos into one single image that has the great sky and nicely exposed car (don't worry, it's easier than you'd think).

Step 10:

We paint with light using a layer mask, and the reason we do it this way is because a layer mask is very forgiving—if you make a mistake, you can instantly paint the mistake away, and no change you make is ever permanent as long as you keep your layer mask. If this doesn't make sense, it will in about three minutes. To add a layer mask to your currently selected layer (your top layer in this case), just click on the Add Layer Mask icon at the bottom of the Layers panel (circled in red here). Your mask will appear as a solid white thumbnail to the right of your image thumbnail in the Layers panel.

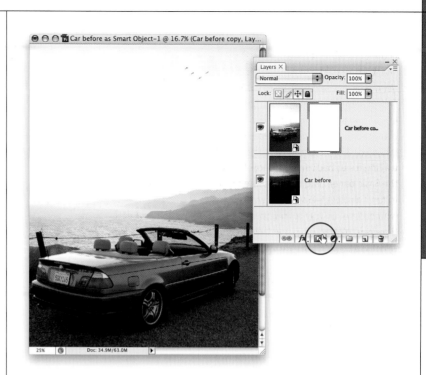

Step 11:

Since your layer mask is white, you'll want to paint on it in the opposite color: black. So, first make sure your Foreground color is set to black, and the quickest way to do this is to just press the letter X, which swaps the Background and Foreground colors. So, press X to make black your Foreground color, and then press B to get the Brush tool. In the Options Bar, click on the Brush tool's thumbnail and choose a medium-sized, soft-edged brush from the Brush Picker. Begin painting over the sky, and as you paint, you'll reveal the darker sky from the original layer below (as shown here). You are, effectively, painting with light as you paint in a darker, more pleasing sky.

Step 12:

Continue painting with this brush until most of the darker sky, water, and mountains in the background are painted in (as shown here), but stop just short of actually painting over the car itself. The reason you need to stop is your brush is too big. When you get close to the car, you'll have to shrink your brush way down to be able to paint right up to it—and right along its edges—but not over it, because then it would reveal the darker version of the car from the bottom layer.

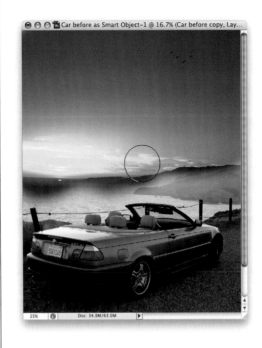

Step 13:

So, either go up to the Brush Picker in the Options Bar and pick a much smaller brush, or do what I do: use the Left and Right Bracket keys to change your brush size. Press the Left Bracket key ([) to make your brush size smaller, or press the Right Bracket key (]) to make it larger (by the way, the Bracket keys are found to the immediate right of the letter P on your keyboard). Make your brush nice and small, be patient, and paint right up to the edge of the car's headrests, then inside the windshield, and then anywhere else that needs to have the darker sky up against it. If you make a mistake, just switch your Foreground color to white (press the letter X again) and paint over the mistake (this covers up your mistake, and is part of the wonder and magic that is a layer mask). Then, switch back to black and continue painting.

Step 14:

Now you get to make a creative decision. Once you've totally painted in the new sky, if you think the car looks too bright to realistically fit in this scene (it looks a little bright to me), then you can "dial in" the right amount of light. You do that by going to the Layers panel and dragging the Opacity slider of this top brighter layer to the left (as shown here, where I thought it looked better at just 70% opacity). Again, this is a creative call that only you, the photographer or retoucher, can make, so it's totally up to you on a photo-by-photo basis. If you like the way it looks at 100%, leave it at 100% (trust me—you'll still be able to sleep at night).

Step 15:

The focus of this photo is clearly the car, and the best way to lead the viewer's eye is with brightness (people look at the brightest, or sharpest, things in a photo first). So to make the car stand out a bit more, you could darken the ground around the car, right? You'll do the same thing you did with the sky—just take the Brush tool, with a medium-sized, soft-edged brush, and paint over the ground (as shown here). As you paint, the darker ground from the layer below it is now revealed. Remember, if you make a mistake (let's say you accidentally painted over a wheel, which made it a lot darker), you just press X to switch the Foreground color back to white. Then paint over the wheel to remove the darkening, switch back to black, and continue painting in other areas of the ground. You can also change the Brush tool's opacity in the Options Bar to paint with gray instead of black, if the ground is looking too dark.

LESSON 2

Step 16:

Here's what the image looks like now, with the darker ground painted in around the car. See how the car really grabs your attention now? It's like you used a couple of flashes with large soft-boxes to add just a little kicker of light onto the car. This is what painting with light is all about, and you can see why this has to be one of the seven points. Now, step back and look at the photo, and using the painting with light power you now have, ask yourself, "What do I wish were different in this photo?"

Step 17:

When I look at the photo, I wish the wheels, tires, and well…most of the car itself was still a bit brighter. To do that, we'll create another copy of the original layer, brighten that copy, and paint with light. So, go to the Layers panel and Control-click (PC: Right-click) on the bottom layer, and from the contextual menu that appears, choose New Smart Object via Copy. Now drag that copy to the top of the layer stack and then double-click directly on the layer's thumbnail to open it in Camera Raw. To brighten the highlights, drag the Exposure slider to the right quite a bit (I dragged it to +2.55), and drag the Contrast slider to the right to +41 (as shown here) to make the highlights brighter and shadows stronger. Now click the OK button.

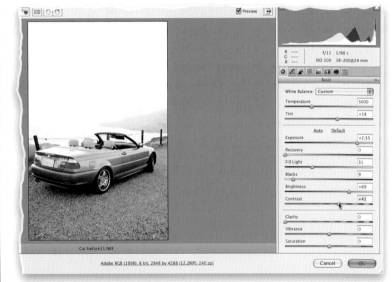

Step 18:

Now you're going to hide that brighter layer behind a layer mask, so press-and-hold the Option (PC: Alt) key and click on the Add Layer Mask icon at the bottom of the Layers panel (as shown here).

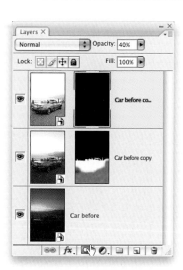

Step 19:

Press X to set your Foreground color to white. Get the Brush tool, choose a small, soft-edged brush from the Brush Picker in the Options Bar, and start painting with light over the wheels and tires (as shown here) to brighten those areas. If they're too bright (and I think they are), just lower the opacity of the layer until it looks right (in this case, it looked right once I lowered the opacity to around 40%).

Step 20:

Now, here's a little twist: you've lowered the opacity of this brighter layer to 40%, but now you want to paint over the side of the car, and when you paint with light over that area, it's too bright. In situations like this, you would lower the opacity of the Brush tool itself instead. In our example, in the Options Bar, I lowered the opacity of the Brush tool to 35%. That way, when you paint over the side of the car, it paints at only 35% of the strength of the rest of the layer (which has been lowered to 40%). This is really handy because it lets you vary the amount of light you paint with in different parts of the same layer.

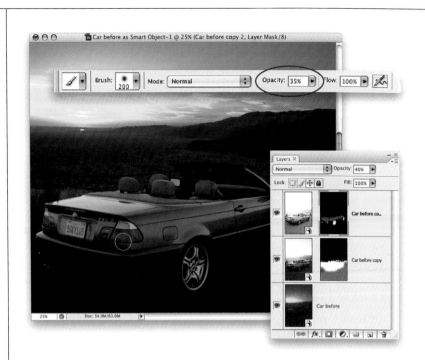

Step 21:

Once you finish painting the side of the car, you need to re-evaluate the brightness of it and see what you think. Here, it seems like the car is still a little too bright overall, so you can lower the opacity of this bright layer even further—down to 20% (as shown here). Now it looks much more natural. You can turn the visibility of this layer on/off by clicking on the little Eye icon to the left of the layer's thumbnail. As you show/hide this layer, you'll see what a difference that little bit of painting with light did for the overall look of the image.

Step 22:

Although the car looks balanced in the scene, we now have a new problem—the whole photo looks a bit too light. Press Command-Option-Shift-E (PC: Ctrl-Alt-Shift-E), which creates a new layer that contains a flattened version of your multi-layered document (look over in the Layers panel at this new layer's thumbnail—it looks just like it would if you flattened the image). To make your entire image darker, you simply change the blend mode of this new layer to Multiply (as shown here), which makes the entire photo much darker. Now, to dial in just the right amount of darkening, you just lower the opacity of this Multiply layer until it looks right (as shown here, where I lowered the Opacity setting to 30%).

Step 23:

Now that our photo is a bit darker overall, let's give it more of that daybreak feel by adding more of a violet tint. You do this by clicking on the Create New Adjustment Layer icon at the bottom of the Layers panel (it's the half-black/half-white circle icon) and choosing Photo Filter. When the Photo Filter dialog appears, choose Violet from the Filter pop-up menu and click OK. That's it—you've added a violet tint to your photo. (*Note:* We generally use this Photo Filter adjustment to warm up a photo [giving it a yellow or orange filter, like a traditional warming filter] or to make a photo cooler [by adding a cooling filter]. Because we chose a very violet-like white balance back in Camera Raw, adding more violet makes sense here, but the color of the light is a creative choice and now we're getting very creative.)

Step 24:

If you think we've gone too far with our violet look, you can bring things back to normal with just one click—addressing both the white balance and Photo Filter creative changes. Here's how: Click on the Create New Adjustment Layer icon at the bottom of the Layers panel and choose Curves. When the Curves dialog appears, click on the center Eyedropper at the bottom of the dialog, and click once on something in your photo that's supposed to be a neutral gray (like the side of the gray car—as we did here). That balances the color and gives you more of a sunset feel. It doesn't get much easier than that. So, now you can choose which of these two looks you like the best—the violet sunrise look from the previous step, or the warmer sunset look you now see here. We'll continue on assuming you decided to stick with the warmer sunset look.

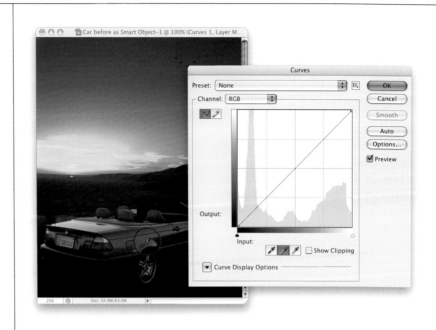

Step 25:

Every photo we bring into Photoshop gets sharpened, and we do this near the end of the process. In this example, we're going to use this photo in a print ad for a local car dealer, so we want to "sharpen for print," which means we're going to sharpen the image so it looks a little too sharp onscreen. When it looks a little too sharp on your screen, it's just right for print, because you lose some of your sharpening in the transfer from backlit image onscreen to reflective image on paper. So, first flatten the image by clicking on the triangle in the top right of the Layers panel and choosing Flatten Image from the flyout menu. Then, under the Filter menu, under Sharpen, choose Unsharp Mask and enter the settings seen here.

Step 26:

Applying high levels of sharpening can cause its own problems. If you don't do it right, halos can appear around your edges, and your image quality starts to suffer. That's why, immediately after applying the Unsharp Mask filter, you'll go under the Edit menu and choose Fade Unsharp Mask. When the Fade dialog appears, change the Mode to Luminosity (to avoid sharpening the color in your photo, where most sharpening problems occur). Then, use the Opacity to apply all or just some of the sharpening.

Before

After

Step 27:

Here you see the Before image (on the left) and the After image (on the right). To finish off the print ad, I added some text by choosing the Horizontal Type tool (T) from the Toolbox. I used the font Helvetica Regular, and I tightened the space between the letters to give the text a more professional, ad agency look (this is done in the Character panel, found under the Window menu, by adding a negative number in the Tracking field—like –15 or –25).

① ADOBE CAMERA RAW PROCESSING
② CURVES ADJUSTMENTS
③ SHADOW/HIGHLIGHT
④ PAINTING WITH LIGHT
⑤ CHANNELS ADJUSTMENTS
⑥ LAYER BLEND MODES & LAYER MASKS
⑦ SHARPENING TECHNIQUES

LESSON 3

This is a shot taken by my buddy Dave Moser after an early morning shoot at a photo workshop in Lake Tahoe, Nevada. Dave had seen this old gas pump behind the Ranger Station earlier that day, but now since the light was already bad, he wasn't going to shoot it (but did anyway). When he saw the photo later, he wished he had shot at f/2.8 or f/4 to blur the background and make the gas pump stand out, and he wished he had shot it earlier to get warmer light and the more saturated colors that were there when he first saw it just after dawn.

LESSON 3

Step One:
Here's the original, unadjusted JPEG photo I talked about above. Dave had his camera's white balance set to Daylight, so when he walked over and shot this gas pump, the whole photo had a bluish tint. The shot is also under-exposed, and again, Dave wishes he had used a wide-open aperture to throw that background a little out of focus, to visually separate the gas pump from the busy and somewhat distracting background. So, we're going to address all of those problems in Photoshop.

DAVE MOSER

Step Two:

We're going to start by opening the Gas Pump JPEG in Camera Raw to make our basic exposure and white balance adjustments. The way you open a JPEG in Camera Raw is to go under Photoshop's File menu and choose Open (PC: Open As), then navigate to where you have the photo on your computer and choose it. Then choose Camera Raw from the Format (PC: Open As) pop-up menu at the bottom center of the dialog (as shown circled here in red), and click Open.

Step Three:

Here's the Gas Pump photo open in Camera Raw, and if the white balance needs adjusting, that's the first thing I adjust. So, to warm the photo up a bit, in the Basic panel, click-and-drag the Temperature slider to the right towards yellow (as shown here, where I dragged to +19), which instantly replaces that cold bluish tint with a warmer yellowish tint (as seen here).

Step Four:

Next, let's increase the exposure a bit by dragging the Exposure slider to the right until the exposure looks better (I dragged it to the right until it read +0.65, as seen here). Now, to bring some color saturation back into the photo, I dragged the Blacks slider to the right a bit until the shadow areas were nice and rich (I dragged it to 13). If you look at the histogram in the upper-right corner, you'll see that there's plenty of clipping in the shadow areas, but if you click on the white triangle in the top-left corner of the histogram, you'll see that the shadow clipping doesn't appear in any areas of critical detail, and if that's the case, we don't worry about it—what's important is how the overall photo looks, not if you have detail in low-detail or low-interest areas.

Step Five:

There is a little highlight clipping and that's easy enough to fix—just drag the Recovery slider a little bit to the right (I only had to drag over to 5) to recover the lost highlights (take a look at the right side of the histogram—there's a gap on the far-right side, between the end of the histogram and the right wall. Since the graph doesn't touch the wall, there's now no clipping in the highlights. If you look back to Step Four, you'll see that the graph does touch, and that the highlight clipping warning in the top-right corner of the histogram is on).

Step Six:

That's really all the adjustments we need to make in Camera Raw, so click on the Open Image button to open the photo in Photoshop itself (as shown here). You can see that the white balance has been changed to warm the photo up, the exposure is better, and the colors are a bit more saturated.

Step Seven:

To really make the colors "pop," we're going to use a Lab color trick I originally learned from color genius Dan Margulis. You convert to Lab color by going under the Image menu, under Mode, and choosing Lab Color (as shown here). This is a non-destructive move, so don't worry—no pixels will be harmed during this experiment.

Step Eight:

Now go under the Image menu and choose Apply Image. When the Apply Image dialog appears, change the Blending pop-up menu to Soft Light (as seen here), and then from the Channel pop-up menu, you're going to try three different channels and see which one looks the best: the Lab channel, the "a" channel, or the "b" channel (the Lightness channel never looks good, so you can just ignore that). That's it—try Lab, "a," then "b," and simply decide which looks better to you (personally, for this image, I liked the way the "b" channel looked, because it added contrast, warmed up the yellow, and added more color saturation. Actually, all three channels did that—I just happened to like "b" the best of the three). When you make your choice (Choose b! Choose b!), click OK.

Step Nine:

Now that our colors are saturated, let's blur the background. Start by pressing Command-J (PC: Ctrl-J) to duplicate the Background layer. You could use the Gaussian Blur filter on this layer, but if you're willing to go that extra step, I'd recommend the Lens Blur filter instead (shown here), because the blur it creates looks more like a traditional blur from a lens than the Gaussian Blur. You'll find the Lens Blur filter under the Filter menu, under Blur. When the Lens Blur filter dialog appears, increase the Radius amount (the blur amount) until the background looks a bit blurry, but you can still make out what it is (like the image shown here, where I dragged to 60), then click the OK button. The Lens Blur filter isn't the fastest filter in the bunch, so you might get a "sit and wait" status bar onscreen while it's doing its thing.

Step 10:

Now you're going to hide that blurry layer behind a black mask so you can "paint with blur" (just like "painting with light") on only the background areas. You do this by pressing-and-holding the Option (PC: Alt) key and then clicking on the Add Layer Mask icon at the bottom of the Layers panel (as shown here). This adds a black layer mask and hides that blurry layer behind it.

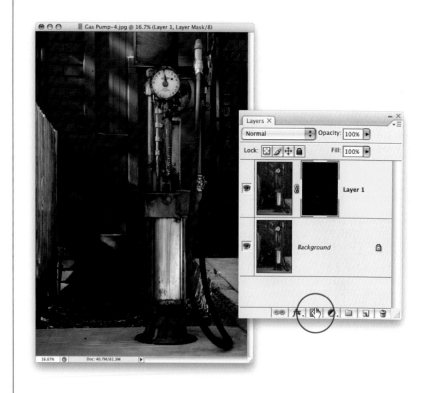

Step 11:

Press X to set your Foreground color to white, press B to get the Brush tool, choose a medium-sized, soft-edged brush from the Brush Picker (up in the Options Bar), and begin painting over the background areas (as shown here, where I'm painting over the background to the pump's left). As you paint, you're revealing the lens-blurred layer from behind that black mask. You are, effectively, using the exact same technique as "painting with light," but instead you're "painting with blur."

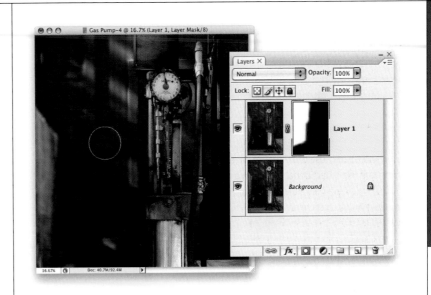

Step 12:

There are two things you're going to have to deal with in painting in this background: (1) You're going to have to shrink your brush way down to be able to paint right up to the pump—and right along its edges. Just be careful not to paint over any part of the pump, because that would reveal the blurry version of the pump. If you do make a mistake, then just press X to switch your Foreground color to black, paint over your mistake (which makes the area you're painting over non-blurry), then switch back to white and continue on. The other thing is (2) as you paint closer to the front of the image, there can't be as much blur, right? As you paint closer up (like I did here), you'll want to lower the Opacity setting of your brush (up in the Options Bar), so you paint with less blur in this area (I lowered mine to 50% when I was getting close, and then 20% when I was really close).

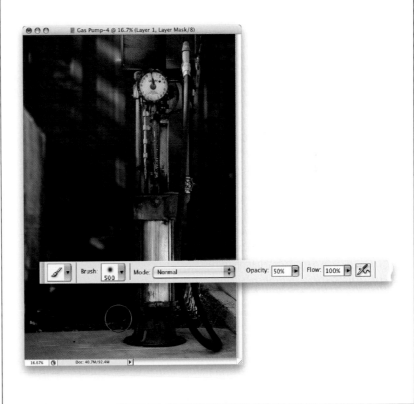

Step 13:

Continue painting with this brush until the background areas are all blurred (as shown here). If the background looks too blurry once you've got it all painted in, you can lower the Opacity setting of the entire layer (at the top right of the Layers panel), and this lowers the amount of blurring on the background. Then, go ahead and flatten the image at this point, because it's time to apply some serious sharpening. To do this, click on the little triangle at the top right of the Layers panel to open the panel's flyout menu, and choose Flatten Image.

Step 14:

Go under the Filter menu, under Sharpen, and choose Unsharp Mask. We can use a higher amount of sharpening on this image because the subject is made up of metal and other well-defined edges that just soak up the sharpening. In other words: this photo is begging to be sharpened. It lives for lots of sharpening, so don't be shy. Here I used an Amount of 120%, a Radius of 1.0, and a Threshold of 3, which gives a nice, crisp amount of sharpening, but in a case like this, I'd probably apply this filter with those same settings twice in a row. Before you apply that second helping, go under the Edit menu and choose Fade. When the Fade dialog appears, change the Mode to Luminosity (so the sharpening is just applied to the detail in the photo, and not the color). Now you can apply the second round of sharpening (if you want), but remember to Fade after you apply the second round.

Step 15:

Next, we're going to draw attention to the gas pump by darkening the background areas. You do this by choosing Levels from the Create New Adjustment Layer pop-up menu at the bottom of the Layers panel. When the Levels dialog appears, click-and-drag the center gray (midtones) Input Levels slider to the right to darken the midtones. Then, at the bottom of the dialog, click-and-drag the white Output Levels slider (on the far right) back over to the left a bit to darken the overall image, then click OK. Because this is all being done on an adjustment layer, it comes with its own built-in layer mask, which we'll make use of in the next step.

Step 16:

At this point, the entire scene is darkened, but we want the gas pump to be nicely lit, so we're going to reveal light on just the gas pump itself by basically painting a stroke of light (what you're really doing is knocking a hole out of the darker adjustment layer). So, press X to set black as your Foreground color, grab the Brush tool, choose a large, soft-edged brush, then paint a stroke from the top of the gas pump down to the bottom (as shown here—you can see the stroke in the adjustment layer's mask thumbnail). You can paint over any areas you think need lightening (as I did here, where I'm repainting over the center of the pump to make sure it's good and light).

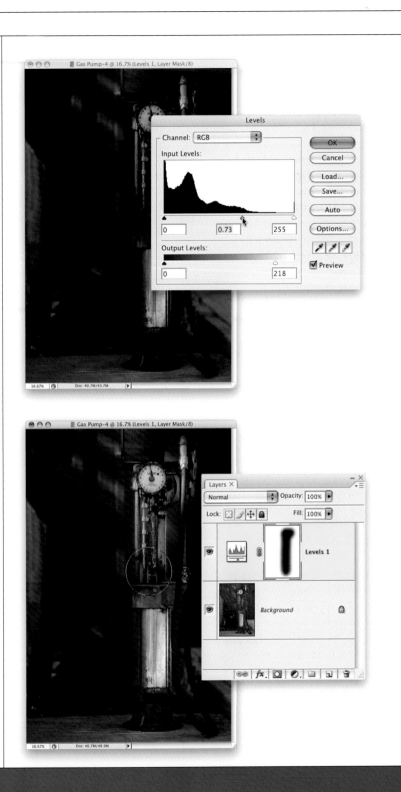

Step 17:

Go ahead and flatten the document. Now, sit back and look at the photo. What do you wish were different? When I look at this image, I wish the face of the round white gauge was brighter, and I wish some other parts of the pump were brighter. I could do another Levels adjustment, and instead of darkening the midtones, I could brighten the highlights, but this might be quicker: duplicate the Background layer, and change this layer's blend mode (at the top left of the Layers panel) to Screen. This brightens the entire photo. Now we're going to hide this brighter layer behind a black mask (you know the routine), so press-and-hold the Option (PC: Alt) key and click on the Add Layer Mask icon at the bottom of the Layers panel.

Step 18:

Once your brighter Screen layer is hidden behind the black mask, get a small, soft-edged brush, press X to set your Foreground color to white, and paint over just the areas you want to be brighter (here I painted over the white, round face of the main gauge, the red base of the pump, and the center area with all those gears). Once again, you're painting with light.

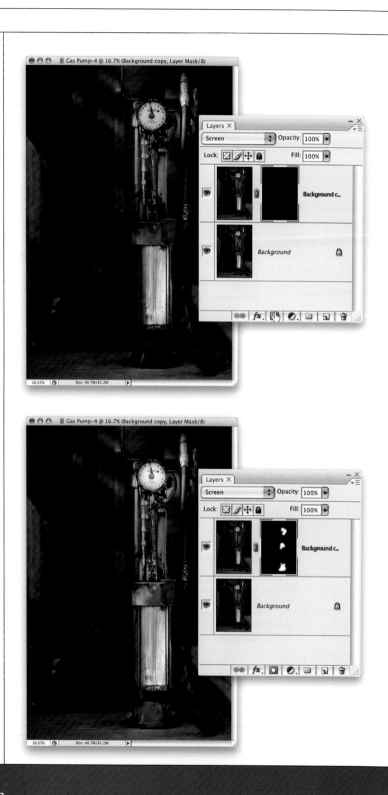

Step 19:

Now that you've controlled where the brighter light will fall (on the face, the base, and the center), you can control the amount of light (the strength of the light) by lowering the Opacity setting for this layer (as shown here, where I lowered the opacity to 60%). That's it! Now compare the original JPEG image (below left), with the one where we fixed the white balance and exposure in Camera Raw, sharpened the photo, blurred the background, and redirected the light so it falls right where we want it, in the amount we want it (below right).

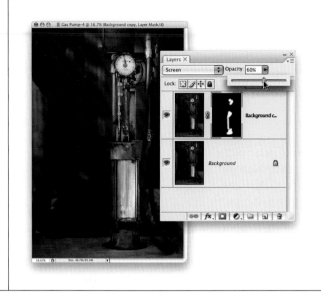

Before

After

LESSON 4

It doesn't look like it, but I took this shot right around dusk on my way to a tiny airport in Page, Arizona, to meet my buddy Matt's flight. When I opened it in Photoshop, I was surprised to see it didn't look nearly as warm as it did when I took the shot, and I was disappointed that the water looked so, well…lame. We'll use the 7-Point System to fix the exposure and color balance problems, but we'll use a good ol' bit of Photoshop magic to make the water look the way we wish it had.

Step One:
Here's the original, unadjusted image opened in Camera Raw. Now, normally we would start by adjusting the white balance for the image, but in this case the photo is so underexposed that we'll need to fix that exposure problem first, so we can clearly see the white balance changes we're making.

SCOTT KELBY

Step Two:
Start by increasing the Exposure setting to around +1.25 to brighten the highlight exposure. Now that you've got a better exposure, you can go back and adjust the white balance. In this case, to make the photo look a little warmer, drag the Temperature slider to the right (as shown here, where I dragged it to 6100).

Step Three:

The photo looks pretty flat, so to increase the saturation in the color and make the shadows richer, drag the Blacks slider to the right until the shadow areas look good to you. I like really rich shadows and nice saturated colors, so I dragged the Blacks slider to 25.

Step Four:

Although the highlights and shadows look much better, increasing the shadows that much made the mountains at the back of the lake too dark. Luckily, that's an easy fix—just drag the Fill Light slider to the right until those mountain areas lighten up (I dragged it over to 17).

Step Five:

Now that we've made all these adjustments, the image looks much better, but
now it looks a little too dark overall. So,
we're going to go back and increase
the overall exposure just a little bit by
dragging the Exposure slider to the right
(as shown here, where I increased the
Exposure setting from +1.25 to +1.45).
The photo looks pretty decent at this
point, so click the Open Image button at
the bottom of the window and we'll continue on in Photoshop.

Step Six:

Once the photo's open in Photoshop,
we're going to deal with the next thing
we wish were different—the water looks
boring. It's not glassy enough to give us
a good reflection, and it doesn't have
enough ripples or waves to look interesting. It's just incredibly "blah" water,
but you're going to fix that. Get the
Rectangular Marquee tool (M) from the
Toolbox and make a selection from the
bottom of the mountains (right where
the mountains meet the lake) on up to
the top of the screen (as shown here).
Basically, you're selecting the top two-
thirds of the photo—just make sure the
bottom of your rectangle is right along
that lake line (as seen here).

Step Seven:

Once your selection is in place, press Command-J (PC: Ctrl-J) to put that selected area up on its own separate layer. Now press Command-T (PC: Ctrl-T) to bring up Free Transform, then Control-click (PC: Right-click) within the selected two-thirds of your image and choose Flip Vertical from the contextual menu.

Step Eight:

This flips your layer vertically (as seen here). To lock in your flip, just press the Return (PC: Enter) key.

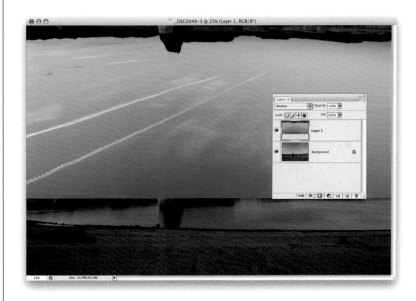

Step Nine:

Switch to the Move tool (V), press-and-hold the Shift key, and drag this flipped layer straight downward until the top of that layer meets the bottom of the mountains, which creates the "reflected in glass-like water" look you see here. By the way, the reason we held the Shift key when dragging was to keep your image perfectly aligned while you were dragging it.

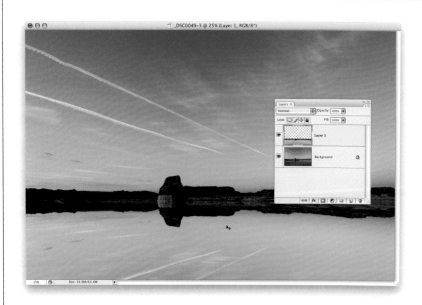

Step 10:

Go to the Layers panel and hide that flipped layer from view by clicking on the Eye icon in the first column. Now, you'll need to put a selection around the lake, and you can use any selection tool (or tools) you feel comfortable with. I used the Magnetic Lasso tool (press Shift-L until you have it), which did a pretty good job of selecting the lake for me. You just click once on the edge of the lake (I started on the lower-right side), then release the mouse button and move slowly along the edge of the lake, and the tool snaps to the edges as if it was magnetic (that's how it got its name). Once you've gone all the way around the lake, you'll probably have to go back and add in any little areas the Magnetic Lasso tool missed by pressing-and-holding the Shift key and using the regular Lasso tool (press Shift-L until you have it) to add in this area. To remove any areas that got selected that you didn't want selected, press-and-hold the Option (PC: Alt) key and draw a selection around those areas until just the lake is selected (as shown here).

Step 11:

With the top layer still selected (your flipped layer), make it visible again by clicking where the Eye icon used to be. Your selection will still be in place (as seen here).

Step 12:

Now, at the bottom of the Layers panel, click on the Add Layer Mask icon (as shown here), which masks your flipped reflection of the sky into the lake selection (if you look in the Layers panel, you'll see the black mask added to your layer). So now you've got beautiful reflective water in the lake, and you can flatten the image by choosing Flatten Image from the Layers panel's flyout menu.

Step 13:

Let's now darken the top of the sky as if you had used a neutral density gradient filter on the photo when it was taken (this is my way of saying, "I should have used a neutral density gradient filter when I took the photo"). Return your Foreground and Background colors to their default black and white settings by pressing the letter D on your keyboard. Then, click on the Create New Adjustment Layer icon at the bottom of the Layers panel (it's the half-black/half-white circle) and choose Gradient. When you do this, it darkens the ground and gradually lightens as your gradient moves up to the sky. This is exactly the opposite of what you want.

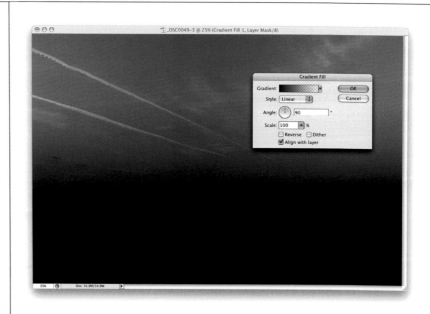

Step 14:

What you want is a darkened sky graduating down to the ground, where your gradient is 100% transparent. To do this—to reverse your gradient—just turn on the Reverse checkbox in the Gradient Fill dialog (as shown here) and click OK.

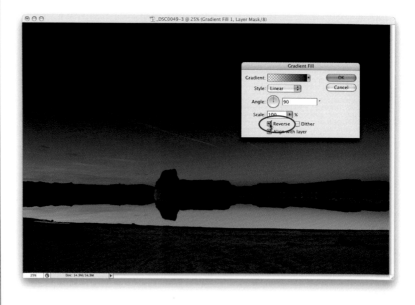

Step 15:

Now, to get this gradient to blend in with your photo, at the top left of the Layers panel, change the blend mode of the Gradient Fill layer to Soft Light (as shown here).

Step 16:

Once you change the blend mode to Soft Light, you'll see the image again—your sky is much darker up top, and it gradually lightens as it moves closer to the ground and the bottom of your image area. If it looks too dark, you can always lower the opacity of this Gradient Fill layer at the top right of the Layers panel.

Step 17:

Go ahead and flatten the document by clicking on the triangle at the top right of the Layers panel and choosing Flatten Image from the flyout menu. Now when I look at the image, it looks like the mountains are a little too dark. If we lightened them, not only will it make them stand out more, it will separate them visually from the reflection in the lake. (*Note:* Whenever I do a reflection technique like this, I usually either darken the reflection or lighten the subject—in this case the mountains.) We're going to use Photoshop's Shadow/Highlight control, but we're going to turn it into the next best thing to an adjustment layer so we can paint with light using the brightened version of the photo. To do this, start by going under the Filter menu and choosing Convert for Smart Filters.

Step 18:

Once you convert your Background layer for Smart Filters, go under the Image menu, under Adjustments, and you'll see that almost everything is grayed out, except for Shadow/Highlight.

Step 19:

Choose Shadow/Highlight and it brings up the Shadows/Highlights dialog (seen here). Adobe assumes that if you need this dialog, you need your shadows opened up, so by default it opens up the shadows by 50% (which, to me, usually seems like way too much). So, lower the Shadows Amount to 0%, then slowly drag the Shadows Amount slider to the right until the mountains start to lighten and more details are clearly visible (as shown here, where I dragged it to 17).

Step 20:

When you click OK, it applies your Shadow/Highlight adjustment as a Smart Filter. If you look in the Layers panel, you'll see that a layer mask has been added below your photo, but it's tied to that layer (that's the way Smart Filters work). The Shadow/Highlight control brightened the shadows in the entire image, and we only wanted to lighten the mountains. So click on the Smart Filters thumbnail to select it (you'll see a black outline around the corners) and press Command-I (PC: Ctrl-I). This inverts the mask to black and covers the Shadow/Highlight effect, which lightened your shadow areas (so, now your photo looks just like it did before you applied the Shadow/Highlight adjustment).

Step 21:

Now you're going to apply those bright-ened shadows only to the mountains by revealing the brighter version using a brush. Start by pressing X to set your Foreground color to white and pressing B to select the Brush tool. In the Options Bar, click on the brush thumbnail and choose a small, soft-edged brush from the Brush Picker. Start painting along the mountain line in the photo, being careful not to paint on the water or sky—just carefully paint over the row of mountains (as shown here).

Step 22:

Once those mountains look brighter and their shadows more open, flatten the image (choose Flatten Image from the Layers panel's flyout menu). We've done all of our edits at this point, so now all we have left to do is apply our sharpening. Go under the Filter menu, under Sharpen, and choose Unsharp Mask. This is a landscape shot with lots of well-defined edges, so you can get away with some nice crisp sharpening. Try Amount: 120%, Radius: 1.0, and Threshold: 3, and then click OK.

Step 23:

Once the sharpening has been applied, go under the Edit menu and choose Fade Unsharp Mask. When the Fade dialog appears, change the Mode to Luminosity (as shown here) to apply the sharpening to just the luminosity in the image, rather than the color (it's the color where most of the sharpening problems occur). The final before and after images are shown below.

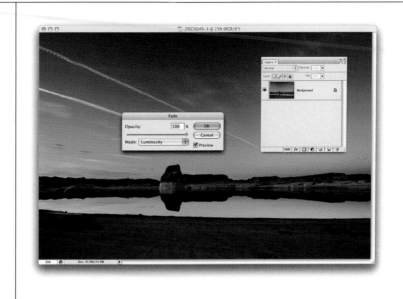

Before

After

1 —— ADOBE CAMERA RAW PROCESSING

2 —— CURVES ADJUSTMENTS

3 —— SHADOW/HIGHLIGHT

4 —— PAINTING WITH LIGHT

5 —— CHANNELS ADJUSTMENTS

6 —— LAYER BLEND MODES & LAYER MASKS

7 —— SHARPENING TECHNIQUES

LESSON 5

All right, you're four lessons into the system and by now you're starting to see a pattern emerge on how this all works. I do want to note that while you must start with Camera Raw as your first step, and you should finish with sharpening as your last, if you put a Curves adjustment before a Shadow/Highlight adjustment (or vice versa), it won't kill the photo correction process, so don't sweat that too much. Just keep doin' what you're doin' for now. This shot was taken at Our Lady of Guadalupe Church during a shoot while I was teaching at the Santa Fe Workshops in Santa Fe, New Mexico.

LESSON 5

Step One:
Open the unadjusted photo (as shown here, where it's a RAW image opened in Camera Raw).

Step Two:
To warm up the building a little, move the White Balance Temperature slider to the right toward yellow, as shown here (I dragged it over to 7600).

SCOTT KELBY

Step Three:

To increase the saturation in the colors in the building, drag the Blacks slider to the right. I dragged it quite a ways (to 41) to get the building looking good (the sky looks really bad, but we'll deal with that later. For now, just worry about making the building look good).

Step Four:

To give the building a little more "snap," drag the Clarity slider to the right a little bit (this adds contrast to the mid-tones and makes the midtone areas look sharper).

Step Five:

We're going to need to double-process this file—once for the building and then again to get a decent exposure in the sky. The quickest way to do this is by opening this photo in Photoshop as a Smart Object. To do that, just press-and-hold the Shift key and you'll see that the Open Image button at the bottom right of the Camera Raw window changes to Open Object. So when you click it (go ahead and click it now), the photo will open in Photoshop as a Smart Object.

Step Six:

When the photo opens in Photoshop, the way you can tell that it's a Smart Object is by the little curled-page icon in the lower-right corner of the layer's thumbnail. To be able to double-process this photo, first Control-click (PC: Right-click) near the layer's name in the Layers panel. When the contextual menu appears, choose New Smart Object via Copy. This makes a duplicate of your Smart Object layer that's not tied to the original (meaning, you can edit this new layer without the changes you make to it being mimicked in the original layer).

Step Seven:
Here's the duplicated Smart Object layer. Now, to reprocess this duplicate in Camera Raw, just double-click directly on the layer's thumbnail (as shown here).

Step Eight:
This duplicate Smart Object opens in Camera Raw, so we can reprocess the photo. Start by dragging the Temperature slider to the left to make the gray sky more blue (here I dragged it to 6400). Now, drag the Exposure slider to the left to darken the exposure of the sky (as seen here, where I dragged it to –0.95).

Step Nine:

When you click OK, you return to Photoshop and your duplicate Smart Object layer is updated with your darker, reprocessed version. Now, you'll need to combine the darker sky from this layer with the better-exposed building on the original layer. We could add a layer mask and paint with light (painting in the darker sky), but with a simple photo like this, we can try a very cool trick. Start by double-clicking on the darker sky layer (double-click right near the layer's name, as shown here).

Step 10:

This brings up the Layer Style dialog. To blend this layer with the one beneath it, go to the bottom of the dialog and drag the left (black) Blend If This Layer slider to the right and the building from the bottom layer will blend into your darker sky layer on top. Here's the thing: while this works pretty brilliantly in this case, the transition between the two layers is kind of hard and a bit jaggy. To get around this, before you start dragging that left slider, press-and-hold the Option (PC: Alt) key and then drag. This splits the slider in two, and for some weird reason only known to Adobe, it makes the blending between these two layers nice and smooth. Click OK.

Step 11:

We're going to go the extra mile to keep our layers intact, just in case we have to go back and change something down the road. So, instead of flattening the image before our next round of changes, press Command-Option-Shift-E (PC: Ctrl-Alt-Shift-E), which creates a new layer with a flattened version of your image (as seen here at the top of the layer stack). Now, the window looks a little dark, so we're going to use the Shadow/Highlight adjustment to open up that area, and we're going use a next-best-thing-to-an-adjustment-layer trick by converting this layer into a Smart Filters layer by going under the Filter menu and choosing Convert for Smart Filters (as shown here).

Step 12:

Go under the Image menu, under Adjustments, and choose one of the only things available—Shadow/Highlight.

Step 13:

The default setting in the Shadows/
Highlights dialog opens up the shadow
areas by 50%, but in most cases that is
way too much (and this case is no excep-
tion). So, drag the Shadows Amount
slider to the left to around 20% (as shown
here) and click OK.

Step 14:

When you click OK, it adds your Shadow/
Highlight adjustment to your layer as
a Smart Filter (you can tell it's a Smart
Filter because it adds a thumbnail
indented below your layer, as seen here
in the Layers panel). At this point, the
fully-brightened image is visible, so click
on the white mask thumbnail for your
Smart Filter, and press Command-I (PC:
Ctrl-I) to Invert your mask to black, which
hides that brighter shadow adjustment
behind that black mask.

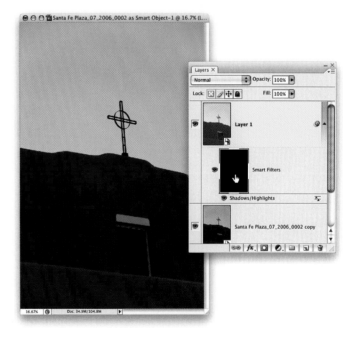

Step 15:

Now press Z to get the Zoom tool and click on the image to zoom in on the window. Press X to set your Foreground color to white, then press B to get the Brush tool, and click on the brush thumbnail in the Options Bar. Choose a medium, soft-edged brush and start painting over the window. As you paint, it reveals the brighter version of your shadow areas. (If you make a mistake while painting, just press X to switch your Foreground color to black and paint over the mistake.)

Step 16:

Continue painting until the entire window has been painted in brighter. *Note:* Besides painting in the brighter version, when the area you want to reveal is made up of straight lines (like this window), another thing you can do is use the Polygonal Lasso tool (press Shift-L until you have it) to select the area around the window. Once your window is fully selected, with your Foreground color set to white, press Option-Delete (PC: Alt-Backspace) to fill your selection with white.

Step 17:

Once you've painted in that area, if it still looks too bright, you can lower the opacity of that layer (which is exactly what I would do [and did] here by lowering the Opacity setting in the top right of the Layers panel to 65%. So…go ahead and do the same thing). Now that our sky is bluer, and the image has some life and contrast, we're going to pump up both the color and contrast at the same time using channels—Lab channels in particular, which is where we turn when we want to add punch to our colors once we're outside Camera Raw.

Step 18:

Your first step is to convert the image to Lab color by going under the Image menu, under Mode, and choosing Lab Color (as shown here). Now, when you do this, you're going to get two warning dialogs that you can totally ignore in this case: (1) the first dialog asks if you want to rasterize your Smart Object layers (turning them into regular layers), which you don't want to do, and (2) the second warning dialog asks if you want to merge the layers (flatten your image), which you also don't want to do. So, hit the Don't button in each dialog. Then press Command-Option-Shift-E (PC: Ctrl-Alt-Shift-E) to create another new layer with a flattened version of your image where we'll add the punch to our colors.

Note: Converting your image into Lab color mode, and then later switching back, doesn't harm your photo—it's a non-destructive move.

Step 19:

Next, go under the Image menu and choose Apply Image. When the dialog appears, in the Blending section at the bottom of the dialog, choose Soft Light from the pop-up menu (as shown here). Now you have a creative choice to make, as there are three possible looks you can get in Soft Light blend mode (or any of the blend modes for that matter): the Lab channel look, the "a" channel look, or the "b" channel look. You can try all three (one at a time) by choosing them from the Channel pop-up menu. In this case, I thought the Lab channel looked the best, but in some cases the "a" channel will look better, or the "b" channel—you have to try all three and see which one looks best to you. When you find the one (choose Lab for this photo), click OK.

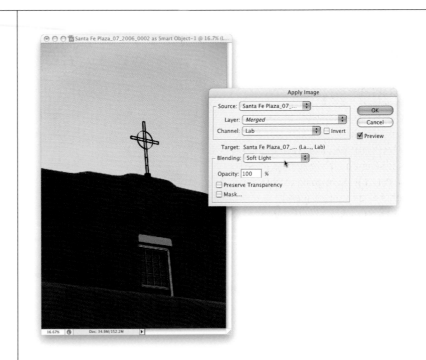

Step 20:

Duplicate the top layer by pressing Command-J (PC: Ctrl-J) and, to make this layer darker, change the blend mode to Multiply (as seen here). Now, you're going to knock out a huge, soft hole in this darker layer, revealing the lighter layers beneath. You do this by first clicking on the Add Layer Mask icon at the bottom of the Layers panel. Then, with your Foreground color set to black, press B to get the Brush tool, and choose a really super-huge brush (like the one you see here, which is 2500 pixels) from the Brush Picker. Take this brush, move over an area of interest in the photo, and just click once. This cuts a very soft-edged hole out of that darker Multiply layer.

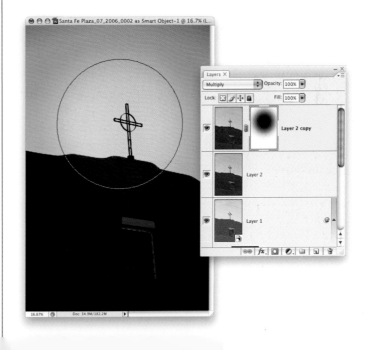

Step 21:

Continue to just click a few times in different areas that you want revealed from the darker version (in the example shown here, I started clicking down by the window, but if you notice I'm pretty much staying away from all the edges of the image and concentrating on the center).

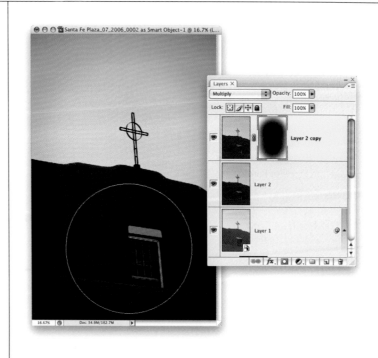

Step 22:

Now that we're at the end of the editing process, we can finally flatten the image (click on the triangle at the top right of the Layers panel and choose Flatten Image from the flyout menu) and then apply our sharpening. Go under the Filter menu, under Sharpen, and choose Unsharp Mask. When the dialog appears, we can use some nice, tight sharpening because of our subject matter, which is made up of well-defined edges (nothing that needs to look soft). So, enter 120% for Amount, set the Radius at 1.0, and the Threshold at 3 (as shown here), and click OK.

Step 23:

As always, when applying sharpening directly to a color photo, right after clicking OK in the Unsharp Mask dialog, go straight to the Edit menu and choose Fade Unsharp Mask (this only appears immediately after you apply the filter. If you do anything else first, this choice won't be available). When the Fade dialog appears, change the Mode to Luminosity (as shown here), which completes your editing process. The before and after images are shown below.

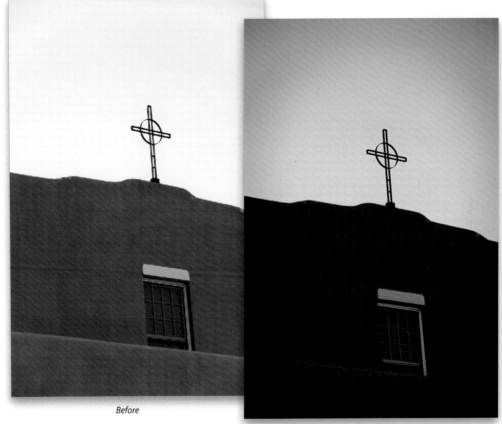

Before

After

LESSON 6

Here we use the system, but we also use some of Photoshop's retouching tools, because even if you fixed the photo's tone and color, the flower damage the insects had done would make it one you'd toss in the trash either way. You can't tell from the photo, but the moment this was taken (in Lake Tahoe, Nevada), a swarm of mosquitoes the size of Rhode Island were attacking me from all sides. I could barely concentrate enough to take the shot because they literally were all over me, so I had to fix this one shot just to prove I survived.

LESSON 6

Step One:

Open the unadjusted original photo. Here, it's a JPEG image of some flowers that are in bad shape, having been dined on by various insects. It's a pretty lame photo, and our goal is to add contrast, make the colors "pop," fix the holes and chomp marks, sharpen and soften the image, and then darken the edges to draw attention away from them. We're going to do this all in Photoshop, so just click the Open Image button here in Camera Raw.

Step Two:

To bring some of the greatly needed contrast back into the image, click on the Create New Adjustment Layer icon at the bottom of the Layers panel (it's the half-black/half-white circle) and choose Curves. When the Curves dialog appears, from the Preset menu at the top, choose Medium Contrast (RGB), as shown here. This creates a curve that basically makes the brighter parts of the image a little brighter, and the darker parts a little darker (which adds contrast).

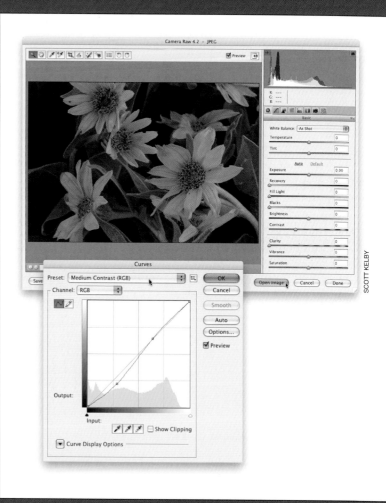

SCOTT KELBY

Step Three:

To add more contrast using Curves is easy—you just make the curve steeper (the steeper the curve, the more intense the contrast). To do that, click once on the third point from the bottom in the curve (the one circled here in red), and then press the Up Arrow key on your keyboard to move this curve point upward (here I pressed it 12 times). This makes the curve steeper and adds more contrast to your photo (as seen here).

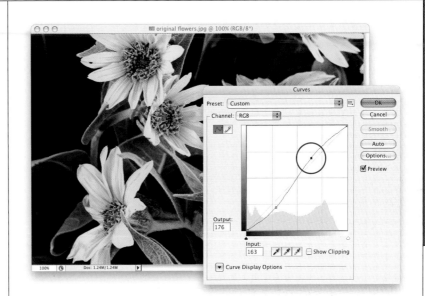

Step Four:

Click OK and you'll see how much more contrast your image now has (compare this image with the one in Step One, and you'll see what I mean). The yellows are brighter, the orange areas in the centers of the flowers are more vivid, the green leaves are more green, and the shadow areas are even darker. Contrast, baby—that's what it's all about!

Step Five:

Go to the Layers panel and click on the Background layer. Now, you're going to get rid of the little spots that appear on the petals and on the leaves. So, get the Healing Brush tool from the Toolbox (press Shift-J until you have it). Next, move the tool over a clean area of petal (one without any spots or other discolorations), then press-and-hold the Option (PC: Alt) key and click once to sample the texture from that area. Now move the Healing Brush over a nearby spot, press the Right Bracket (]) key to make your brush size a little larger than the spot itself, and just click. Don't paint—just click once, and the spot is gone (as shown here, on the two top-right petals on the flower on the right). So take a minute or two, move around the photo, and remove any spots on the petals and leaves.

Step Six:

Now let's fix the chomp marks on the petals. Press Z and click on a petal to zoom in. Get the Elliptical Marquee tool (press Shift-M until you have it) and click-and-drag out an oval-shaped selection over the chomp area (as shown here), making it so the edge of your oval runs right along the edge of the petal (in the example shown here, see how the top center of my oval extends along the line of where the petal would have been if a bite hadn't been taken out of it?). You're doing this because in the next step you're going to cover up that chomp hole by cloning a nearby part of the petal over that spot. When you have a selection in place, Photoshop won't let you paint outside that selection, so you can't accidentally paint outside the lines (so to speak).

Step Seven:

Now press S to switch to the Clone Stamp tool, and move your cursor to a nearby area that has the same color and tone as where you want to repair. Click on the brush thumbnail in the Options Bar and choose a small, soft-edged brush from the Brush Picker. Press-and-hold the Option (PC: Alt) key and click once to sample that area for cloning. Now move your cursor over the repair area and start painting. As you paint, the area you sampled a moment ago gets cloned (copied) over your open chomp hole (as shown here). The plus-sign cursor shows the area you sampled from, and the round brush cursor shows where you're painting. When you're done cloning, just Deselect by pressing Command-D (PC: Ctrl-D).

Step Eight:

Move to another chomp mark and do the same thing—make an oval-shaped selection along the edge of the petal (to keep you from accidentally painting onto the leaves or background), then sample a nearby area and paint with that sampled area over the hole (as seen here).

Step Nine:

This petal, on the bottom of the flower on the top left, is a little trickier (but only a little), because of where the chomp appears (right at the end of the petal), so it's important to continue the little line that comes down the center of the petal. You start the same way, by making an oval-shaped selection over the repair area, and right up to the edge of the petal. But then you'll need to sample directly on the line in the petal. If you look at the cursors shown here, you can see that the sample area plus-sign cursor is positioned right on the line above the selected area, and the round brush cursor is painting over the hole, but right along that same straight-line path. This way it copies the line as you clone and makes it look realistic.

Step 10:

Once you've patched all the chomps in the petals, and removed the major spots on the flowers, take a moment to remove any straggling spots on the green leaves, or anywhere else in the photo. You want to have all this taken care of before you sharpen the photo.

Step 11:

We're going to add a softening technique to this photo, but before you do any softening, you need to do your sharpening first (it's really hard to sharpen an intentionally blurry photo). So in this one particular case, we're going to bend the rules and sharpen before we're really done. Start by clicking on the triangle in the top right of the Layers panel and choosing Flatten Image from the flyout menu to flatten the layers, then go under the Filter menu, under Sharpen, and choose Unsharp Mask. Since our subject is of a softer nature, we'll use a softer amount of sharpening. For Amount choose 85%, for Radius choose 1.0, and for Threshold choose 3, then click OK.

Step 12:

Now, here's a real world scenario for you: you've sharpened the photo and then you step back, look at the image, and wish that the centers of the flowers were darker and more saturated. Of course, you could undo your sharpening, go back a few steps, and address the problem, or you could just bend the rules a bit and go ahead and fix the problem now using Curves. So, how did I determine it was okay to apply a Curves adjustment after sharpening? It was only because I knew that later I would be blurring the image, and that would hide any minor flaws caused by using Curves after the sharpening. That's the only reason we can get away with it. So, choose Curves from the Layers panel's Create New Adjustment Layer pop-up menu. When the Curves dialog appears, click directly in the center (to add a center point), then press the Down Arrow key on your keyboard to darken the midtones (making the centers of the flowers much richer in tone).

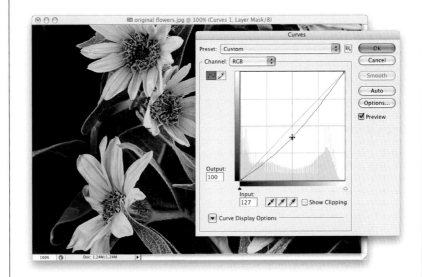

Step 13:

Click OK and your simple midtone adjustment is made and the centers of your flowers are darker, but now so is everything else. Luckily, you used an adjustment layer, so all you have to do is press Command-I (PC: Ctrl-I), and now your darkened midtones are hidden behind a black layer mask (as seen in the Layers panel shown here).

Step 14:

By now you know the routine: press D to set your Foreground color to white, press B to get the Brush tool, click on the brush thumbnail in the Options Bar, grab a medium-sized, soft-edged brush, and paint over the centers of the flowers to reveal the darker version. In the example shown here, I'm painting over (revealing) the darker center on the flower up in the top-left corner.

Step 15:

Go ahead and choose Flatten Image from the Layers panel's flyout menu and flatten these layers now because we're going to soften the image and finish this puppy off. First, press Command-J (PC: Ctrl-J) to duplicate the Background layer, then go under the Filter menu, under Blur, and choose Gaussian Blur. When the dialog appears, enter 5 pixels (for small, low-resolution images, or 20 pixels for high-res images) to put a blur over the entire photo and click OK.

Step 16:

Now, in the Layers panel, simply lower the Opacity setting of this layer to around 35% to give a soft, diffuse effect to the entire image (as seen here). There's just one last thing to do.

Step 17:

Once again, flatten your layers and then press Command-J (Ctrl-J) to duplicate the Background layer. We're going to paint with light here—darken the photo and then reveal the lighter flowers one by one. Start by changing the top layer's blend mode to Multiply (as shown here).

Step 18:

Click on the Add Layer Mask icon at the bottom of the Layers panel. Press X to set your Foreground color to black and press B to get the Brush tool. Click on the brush thumbnail in the Options Bar and choose a really huge, soft-edged brush from the Brush Picker (like the one shown here), and just click once or twice over the top set of flowers. This reveals the brighter version of them from the layer below, almost like the sun just peeked out from behind a cloud.

Step 19:

Click once or twice just over the flowers, or any spot where you'd like light to fall, and you're done (here I clicked about seven or eight times). Lastly, flatten the layers to complete the edit. The before and after images are shown below.

Before

After

LESSON 7

This is a shot where it was a beautiful twilight, I had a great angle of the Golden Gate Bridge, had my camera on a tripod, and a cable release attached. Everything was right on the money—except my exposure. The downside of underexposing a digital photograph is when you increase the exposure, you increase the noise. Luckily, with a quick exposure fix and a little creative white balance adjustment, you're on your way. The challenge is keeping the car lights from getting so bright that they draw your attention away from the bridge and the sky.

LESSON 7

Step One:
Open the unadjusted RAW photo in Camera Raw (as shown here).

SCOTT KELBY

Step Two:

Our first step is to find a better white balance, because in the image you see back in Step One, the sky looks pretty lame. You can see pretty quickly if a white balance change looks good by simply trying each of the built-in White Balance presets in the pop-up menu. Choose Fluorescent from that menu to replace that awful-looking gray/green in the sky with a nice dark blue. *Note:* All these white balance preset choices are only available when processing RAW photos. If this were a JPEG or TIFF image opened in Camera Raw for processing, the only presets would be As Shot or Auto on the White Balance pop-up menu.

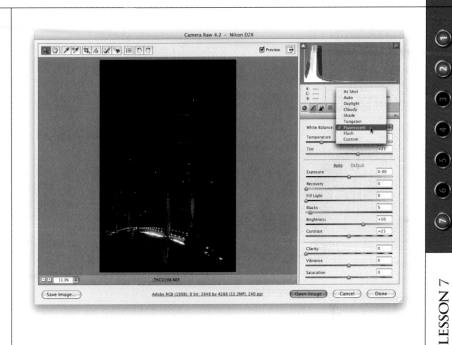

Step Three:

Now, let's make the image brighter by dragging the Exposure slider to the right (as shown here, where I dragged over to +2.40). This brings out some nice gradations of color from the top of the image down to the bridge, where the colors go from dark blue, to a lighter blue, to purple, and then it increases the magenta in the purple.

Step Four:

The downside of this increase in the exposure is that the car lights on the bridge are now really distractingly bright (look back in Step Three and you'll see what I mean). An easy way to fix this is to simply drag the Brightness slider back to the left a bit (I dragged it back to +20 from its default setting of +50). By the way, the Brightness slider controls the midtone areas of the image.

Step Five:

Lastly, to add some snap and punch to the midtones, drag the Clarity slider to the right just a little bit (I dragged over to 17).

Step Six:
To bring out a little more detail in the bridge, drag the Fill Light slider over to the right a bit (I dragged over to 26), which opens up the shadow areas.

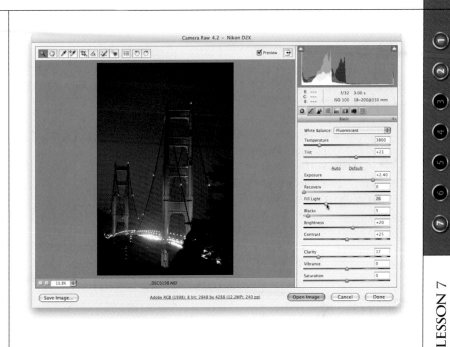

Step Seven:
The last thing we'll do here in Camera Raw is to straighten the photo (I don't know if you noticed how crooked it is, but take a look at the bridge and you'll see—it's leaning a little to the right). Get the Straighten tool (A) from the top tool-bar. Click-and-hold it near the base of the tower closest to you, then drag upward along the side of the tower (as shown here). When you release the mouse button, it puts a cropping rectangle into place that's rotated the exact amount to perfectly straighten your image.

LESSON 7

Step Eight:

Click the Open Image button in Camera Raw, and your cropped (straightened) photo is opened in Photoshop. Now, let's add some more contrast to the photo by choosing Curves from the Create New Adjustment Layer pop-up menu at the bottom of the Layers panel. (*Note:* We could have actually added contrast using the Tone Curve in Camera Raw, but sometimes you don't realize the photo needs extra contrast until later on.) When the Curves dialog appears, choose Medium Contrast (RGB) from the pop-up menu (as shown here) to add a nice bit of contrast to the photo.

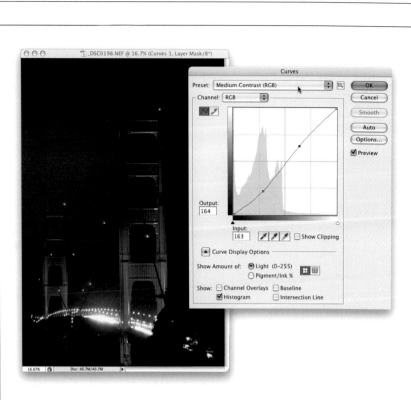

Step Nine:

Now it's time to sharpen and finish this project off. First, choose Flatten Image from the Layers panel's flyout menu to flatten your layers. Then go under the Filter menu, under Sharpen, and apply the Unsharp Mask filter with a higher amount of sharpening based on the subject (the bridge is metal, with lots of well-defined edges). I used Amount: 120%, Radius: 1, Threshold: 4. Now click OK to apply the sharpening.

Step 10:

Then, go under the Edit menu and choose Fade Unsharp Mask, and when the Fade dialog appears, change the Mode pop-up menu to Luminosity, and click OK. The final image and the original are shown below.

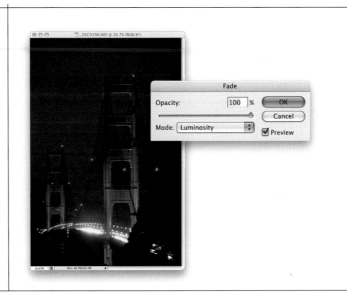

Before

After

LESSON 8

This is a shot of my buddy Matt taken down in Nassau, Bahamas. The background is the rusty hull of an old boat, but the vibrant color of the hull was totally lost thanks to poor exposure, a bad white balance setting, and a few other in-camera mistakes, which you'll fix surprisingly easily using the System. Then you'll use a couple of simple Photoshop "finishing effects" to top things off. Also, we'll really make use of Camera Raw's Clarity and Sharpening controls, along with Photoshop's Unsharp Mask filter, to make this image really crisp and clear.

Step One:

Open the unadjusted photo in Camera Raw (as shown here). Light reflects the color it hits, so when you put your subject next to a wall with vivid colors like this, those colors are going to reflect right back onto your subject. That's why Matt's skin is very yellow (and so is his backpack, and the camera, and well…everything).

SCOTT KELBY

Step Two:

We'll start with a white balance adjustment to get Matt's skin tone back in line (basically, we need to lower the amount of yellow in the photo). To do that, drag the White Balance Temperature slider to the left, toward blue (I dragged it to 4650 here), which removes the yellow color cast from the photo.

Step Three:

Now let's brighten the photo by dragging the Exposure slider to the right (in this case, to +1.15. I stopped before the right side of the histogram hit the right wall—that little gap between the graph and the right wall ensures that we've maintained detail in our highlights). If you look back at Step One, you can see the effect that moving just these two sliders has made in the overall image (of course, we're not done yet—but what a great start).

Step Four:

One area in this photo that looks a little too dark (to me anyway) is the backpack Matt's wearing. There's a lot of cool detail in that backpack, but it's so dark you're losing a lot of it. That's when you reach for the Fill Light slider—it's designed to open up those shadow areas and reveal detail, and this is a great example of when you'd want to use it. Just drag the Fill Light slider to the right (as I have here, dragging it over to 34), which opens up the detail in his backpack, his shirt, and even in the camera he's holding.

Step Five:

Opening up the shadows (using the Fill Light slider) does sometimes have a downside, and that is it tends to wash out the shadows a bit in areas where you didn't need the Fill Light applied (so, the Fill Light helped the backpack, but a lot of other shadow areas got opened up, too). The remedy is easy (we were going to do it anyway as part of our correction process), and that is to increase the Blacks amount. So, drag the Blacks slider to the right, and notice how the whole image looks more balanced now. (*Note:* Be careful not to drag the Blacks slider so far to the right that you undo all the good you did with the Fill Light slider.)

Step Six:

This shot was hand-held near dusk, so it's not a really tack-sharp shot, so we're going to bring as much sharpness into the photo as we can at this stage (while we're still doing our "capture" processing in Camera Raw). The Clarity slider is a great starting point, but before you use this slider, make sure you're viewing your image at 100% (if not, you won't really see the effect of the Clarity control). A quick way to get to a 100% view is to double-click directly on the Zoom tool up on the far left of the Camera Raw toolbar. Now, here's what I recommend: go ahead and drag the Clarity slider all the way over to the right to 100, so you can see how clarity affects your midtone contrast. Then, drag it back to the left until it looks right to you. Because it's somewhat subtle, dragging all the way to 100 first helps you see what you're looking for.

Step Seven:

To add some extra contrast (which helps in getting an overall sharper look), click on the Tone Curve icon at the top of the panel area (the second from the left). Click on the Point tab, and from the Curve pop-up menu, choose Strong Contrast. In the next step, we're going to add "capture sharpening" (to regain some of the original sharpness lost during the capture process). We add this type of sharpening to every photo at this stage (in fact, Camera Raw adds a small amount of sharpening automatically to every photo—just like your camera adds sharpening to JPEG photos while they're in the camera). Now, click on the Detail icon (the third from the left).

Step Eight:

Just like with Clarity, before you start dragging sliders, double-click on the Zoom tool to jump to a 100% view. The Sharpening Amount slider does what you'd expect—it controls the amount of sharpening, and this photo needs plenty. So, drag the Amount slider to the right to 66. Leave the Radius slider set at 1.0 (we rarely increase it above 1.0). The Detail slider is our "halo avoidance slider," which helps us avoid those little halos that can appear around edges when we apply lots of sharpening. Lower numbers provide more halo protection—higher numbers provide less (and 100% gives you close to the effect of Unsharp Mask, which isn't so great). The default setting is 25, but I increased it to 50 to get punchier sharpening for this type of image. (*Tip:* If you press-and-hold the Option [PC: Alt] key as you drag the slider, the image preview turns gray, and shows you how the edges are affected.)

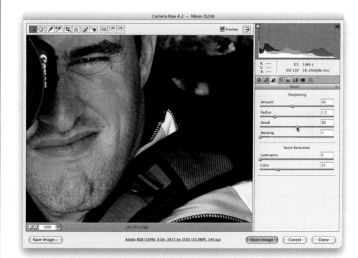

Step Nine:

Now go ahead and click the Open Image button at the bottom right of the window to open the processed photo in Photoshop. Although the tones are much more balanced than when we started, and we've added some additional contrast and sharpening, we need to move to that next level of editing to really finish this photo off, right?

Step 10:

Click on the Create New Adjustment Layer icon at the bottom of the Layers panel (the half-white/half-black circle) and choose Curves from the pop-up menu. Click on the shadow Eyedropper (the one on the left half-filled with black) and click it once on something in the photo that's supposed to be the color black. I thought a pretty safe bet would be the dark area inside the lens on the camera he's holding, so click right there (as shown circled here). This makes the shadow areas neutral.

Step 11:

Now click on the highlight Eyedropper (the one on the right half-filled with white), and click on something in the photo that's supposed to be the color white (or click on the brightest thing in the photo). In this case, it's pretty easy—there's white in his shirt, so we can just take our Eyedropper and click there. I chose to click on the bright area right above his front shoulder. The photo looks better, but unlike when we're in Camera Raw, I don't instantly know whether increasing the highlights like this is going to clip off the details in those areas.

Step 12:

Luckily, in CS3, Adobe added a way to monitor your clipping—you just have to turn it on. To the immediate right of the Eyedropper tools is a checkbox for showing any clipping in the photo. Turn on that checkbox (as shown here), and your image window turns black. Any areas that appear in a color are being clipped (losing detail) in the highlights. In the example shown here, the red areas are just clipping in the Red channel, the yellow areas in the Yellow channel, and anything that appears in solid white is losing detail in all the channels. If these are areas of important detail (and Matt's arm is an area of important detail—well, at least it is to Matt), then you need to choose a different bright spot—a brighter spot than where you clicked before—as your new highlight point (we'll do this in the next step).

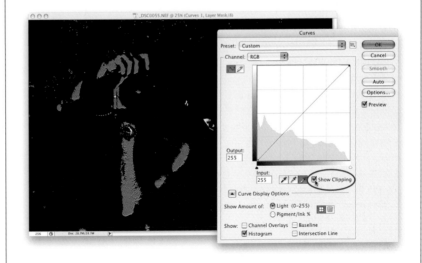

Step 13:

Turn off the Show Clipping checkbox so you can see the full-color image again. Now, take the highlight Eyedropper and click on a different white area (in this case, I clicked the Eyedropper once on the area of white shirt on his waist, as shown here).

Step 14:

The only way to know if the new area you clicked on is better is to turn on the Show Clipping checkbox again (as I did here), and look at the image. As you can see here, the image window is pretty much solid black, which is good (those two tiny green spots aren't anything to worry about), because you've chosen a highlight spot that doesn't damage your highlights. Turn off the Show Clipping checkbox again to return to your full-color image.

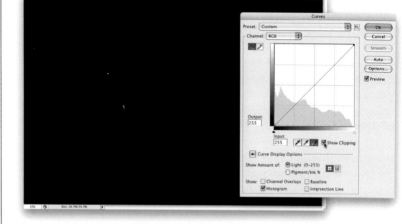

Step 15:
The last thing left to adjust here is the midtones, which you do using the middle Eyedropper that's half-filled with gray. Click on it, then click on something in your photo that's supposed to be a neutral gray. In this case, the camera case backpack that Matt's carrying has plenty of areas that should be gray, so click on one of those areas (as I did—it's circled here in red). You don't have to worry about checking for clipping with midtones. Although it's probably possible to have highlight clipping using the midtone Eyedropper, it's pretty unlikely, so you can just skip it. Before you click OK, turn off the Preview checkbox (under the buttons on the top right), so you can see a before/after of your Curves adjustments. Toggle it back on/off a few times, then click OK to apply your Curves changes.

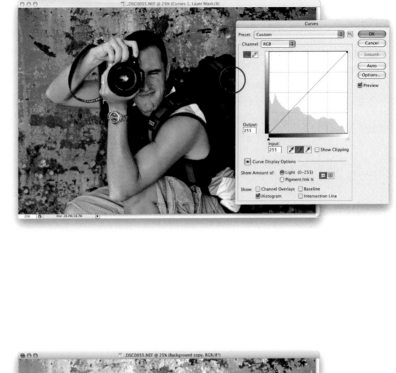

Step 16:
One thing I would do at this point is to paint with light over the areas of the photo that you want to really stand out and have lots of detail. Matt stands out no problem—but I would add additional detail in his backpack, hair, and camera lens. To do this, click on the Background layer, then press Command-J (PC: Ctrl-J) to duplicate the Background layer. Now, at the top left of the Layers panel, change the blend mode of this layer to Screen to make the photo twice as bright (as seen here).

Step 17:

Press-and-hold the Option (PC: Alt) key and click on the Add Layer Mask icon at the bottom of the Layers panel to hide the brighter Screen layer behind a black layer mask (as seen here). Now, with your Foreground color set to white, press B to get the Brush tool. Click on the brush thumbnail in the Options Bar, choose a small, soft-edged brush, and paint over just the areas you'd like to be brighter—like the backpack, the lens, his hair, and any other area you think should be brighter. Again, you're painting with light, applying extra light just where you want it.

Step 18:

I always leave the Opacity setting for this "painting with light on a Screen layer" set to 100% while I'm painting, so I can clearly see the light, even if it's too strong. Then, I go back and lower the opacity of the layer to "dial in" just the right amount of light. So, go to the Layers panel and lower the Opacity setting of this Screen layer to around 45%.

Step 19:

Go ahead and flatten the image (by clicking on the triangle in the top right of the Layers panel and choosing Flatten Image from the panel's flyout menu). Now we're going to add a vignette effect to darken the outer edges of the photo and focus the attention clearly on our subject. Start by duplicating the Background layer by clicking-and-dragging it onto the Create a New Layer icon at the bottom of the Layers panel. Then change the duplicate layer's blend mode to Multiply to darken the entire photo.

Step 20:

Press M to get the Rectangular Marquee tool from the Toolbox, and click-and-drag out a large rectangular selection that's inset an inch or two from the outside edges of your image (as shown here). Then go under the Select menu, under Modify, and choose Feather (we're going to add a feather to greatly soften the edges of this selection).

Step 21:
When the Feather Selection dialog appears, enter 200 pixels, which is a huge amount of softening, and click OK.

Step 22:
Now press the Delete (PC: Backspace) key on your keyboard to knock a soft-edged hole out of your darker Multiply layer, revealing part of the brighter original layer beneath it. The end effect is the edges of your photo appear darker, and then they smoothly blend into a brighter center. This gives the effect of having a soft light shining on your subject, as seen here. You can Deselect by pressing Command-D (PC: Ctrl-D), and with the selection border gone, you can see something we should probably fix—the edge burning looks good everywhere except on Matt's knee, but luckily, that's easy to fix at this stage.

Step 23:

Because the darker edge is on its own layer, we just have to erase the part of that layer that extends over Matt's knee. So, press E to grab the Eraser tool, click on the brush thumbnail in the Options Bar, and then choose a soft, medium-sized brush. Just erase right over his knee area—the darkened part of that layer is erased, and his knee looks back to normal. Now you can go ahead and flatten your layers again.

Step 24:

Now let's apply some final sharpening. This is sharpening (a) we either apply for effect, making the photo sharper than it actually was, or (b) we do what's called "output sharpening," which is where we oversharpen the photo a bit to compensate for the sharpness that's lost during the printing process (if the photo looks a bit too sharp onscreen, it usually looks perfect when printed). In our case, we'll do the standard sharpening (sharpening for effect), and we'll use the Sharpen High action we created in Lesson 1. So go to the Actions panel (from the Window menu, choose Actions if it is not visible), click on Sharpen High, and then click the Play Selection icon at the bottom of the Actions panel (as shown here).

Step 25:

We're now going to pull out a pro-sharpening trick that makes the photo look even sharper than it really is. You start by duplicating the Background layer by clicking-and-dragging it onto the Create a New Layer icon at the bottom of the Layers panel. Then bring up the Unsharp Mask dialog (by going under the Filter menu, under Sharpen, and choosing Unsharp Mask). We're going to intentionally oversharpen this photo (after all, we just sharpened it in the last step, right?) by applying these settings: Amount: 150%, Radius: 1.0, Threshold: 3. Then click OK. Now you've got an oversharpened overall image.

Step 26:

Press-and-hold the Option (PC: Alt) key and click on the Add Layer Mask icon at the bottom of the Layers panel to hide this super-sharpened layer behind a black mask (as seen here).

Step 27:

With your Foreground color set to white, press B to get the Brush tool, click on the brush thumbnail in the Options Bar, and choose a small, soft-edged brush. Paint over just the areas that can hold a lot of sharpening—areas like his watch, the face of the lens (as shown here), and any metal items on his backpack (buckles, snaps, etc.). These types of things can really hold a lot of sharpening. Although you think this might be subtle, once you're done painting over these small areas, turn off the top, super-sharp layer (by clicking on the Eye icon to the left of the image thumbnail in the Layers panel). You'll be amazed at the difference in how much sharper the overall photo looks, even though just these small areas have been super-sharpened.

Before

After

Step 28:

Now you can flatten the image, and check out the overall sharp look of the photo. Also, note how nicely the edges are burned in. If I hadn't pointed it out, most people wouldn't have realized that they were burned in at all, but it really makes a big difference.

LESSON 9

This is an image of a neutral density gradient filter I took for my book, *The Digital Photography Book*. It was taken on a white seamless background using a single overhead softbox. There are lots of problems, including the fact that it was shot on a white seamless background, but it looks like a definitely off-white, yellowish, yucky background, plus you can't see the gradient that is supposed to be visible in the filter, and we had to prop the filter up with a small piece of cardboard, which has to be removed later in Photoshop. Don't worry—it's a piece of cake.

LESSON 9

Step One:
Open the unadjusted original RAW photo in Camera Raw.

SCOTT KELBY

Step Two:
We always start by getting our white balance right, and in this case, since we know the background is supposed to be gray, we can use the White Balance tool. Get it from the toolbar at the top of the Camera Raw window (it's the third icon from the left, or just press I), then click it once in an area that's supposed to be light gray (as shown here), and it sets a custom white balance for you. Couldn't be easier. I use this method (this tool) in situations where I know something in the photo is supposed to be gray—then I'm just one click away from the right white balance.

Step Three:

Now, we don't want to brighten the photo, or our histogram (at the top of the panel area) will hit the right-side wall, which means we'll lose detail. So, let's leave the Exposure slider alone. Instead, let's bring out some detail in the sides of the filter by going to the Fill Light slider and dragging it to the right to open up the dark shadow areas on the back side of the filter (here, I dragged it to 28). The downside of this adjustment is that the nice black gradient at the top of the image is now much lighter (but don't worry—we'll fix that later).

Step Four:

This is a very gray, midtoney photo (the subject doesn't have lots of interesting highlights—it's a gray filter on a gray background), so let's add some punch to the photo by increasing the Clarity amount. This can make a big difference in photos like this. Before you use the Clarity slider, remember to zoom in to a 100% view by either double-clicking on the Zoom tool in the toolbar (the little magnifying glass icon on the left) or by choosing 100% from the Select Zoom Level pop-up menu at the bottom left of the window, as seen here (which is critical when using the Clarity control).

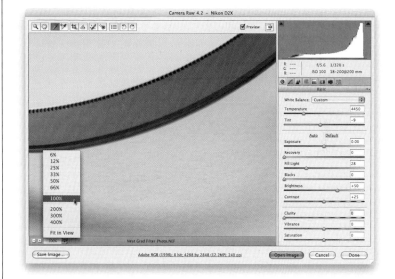

Step Five:

Drag the Clarity slider all the way to the right to 100, so you can clearly see the effect of adding Clarity. Then, drag it back down to 0 (so you can see it off), and then drag back to the right until the edges of the filter look nice and crisp (as shown here, where I dragged it over to 58). As for the capture sharpening, we'll just leave the Sharpening settings (found in the Detail panel) set at their defaults, which does apply some soft overall sharpening.

Step Six:

Remember back in Step Three when we increased the Fill Light amount and it made the top of the black gradient too light, and it even introduced a little bit of a yellowish color cast? And remember how I told you that we'd fix it later? Well, it's now later. Press-and-hold the Shift key and you'll notice that the Open Image button (at the bottom right of the Camera Raw window) has now become the Open Object button. Click that button to open this photo in Photoshop as a Smart Object.

Step Seven:

Now that the photo is open in Photoshop as a Smart Object, we need to make a duplicate of this layer, but we don't want the duplicate tied to our original Smart Object (which is the default behavior for duplicates of Smart Objects). To do this (break the tie), go to the Layers panel and Control-click (PC: Right-click) on the layer, and from the contextual menu that appears, choose New Smart Object via Copy (as shown here).

Step Eight:

When the copy appears in Photoshop, in the Layers panel, double-click directly on the duplicate layer's thumbnail to open it in Camera Raw. When it opens, the settings you last used are still in place, so all you have to do is lower the Fill Light amount back down to 0, and increase the blacks just a little bit (here, I dragged the Blacks slider to 9). That way, your gradient is nice and black again. Now click OK, and you return to Photoshop where your duplicate layer is updated with your change.

Step Nine:

You now have two layers: one (the bottom layer) has the good-looking filter with the too-light gradient at the top, and the top layer has the good gradient, but the filter is too dark. Here's how to quickly combine the best parts of both to create one perfect image: Click on the Add Layer Mask icon at the bottom of the Layers panel. Press D to set your Foreground color to black. Get the Gradient tool (G) from the Toolbox and choose the Foreground to Transparent gradient from the Gradient Picker in the Options Bar. Press-and-hold the Shift key, click just above the filter, and then drag straight upward to the top of the image (as shown here. By the way—the reason you press-and-hold the Shift key is to keep your gradient perfectly straight as you drag).

Step 10:

What this does is leaves just the top part of the top layer visible (the original darker black gradient), but it reveals the original filter from the bottom layer. So what you're seeing is just the top one-quarter of the top layer, and the bottom three-quarters of the bottom layer. If you take a look at the layer mask in the Layers panel, it will help you to see what you did. Remember the old rule: white reveals and black conceals. So the white area revealed the top of the top layer, and the black area concealed the rest of it. Pretty slick when you think about it. Now, this is important: we don't want to flatten yet, so press Command-Option-Shift-E (PC: Ctrl-Alt-Shift-E), which creates a new layer with a flattened version of your photo (so beneath that flattened layer will be the two Smart Object layers you see here).

Step 11:

Now we have to face the biggest challenge here—removing the little piece of cardboard used to hold the filter up at an angle (seen under the right side of the filter). The easiest way is to put a selection around the area you want to erase (so you can't accidentally erase outside that area), then use the Clone Stamp tool to clone the background area over the cardboard. I'd make the selection with the Pen tool, because it's the best tool for the job and it's easy to use. So, press Z and click on the filter to zoom in on the image. Then get the Pen tool (P) from the Toolbox and click once along the edge of the filter (as shown here). Don't click-and-hold—just click once and release the mouse button. (*Note:* Make sure you have the Paths icon active in the Options Bar—it's the second one from the left, circled here in red.)

Step 12:

Next, move your Pen tool cursor over to the other side of the filter—just past the piece of cardboard. Now you're going to click, hold, and drag up. As you drag, a path will appear between the two points and you'll see your path bend around the filter. The farther you drag, the more it bends. Don't release the mouse button until you have the path tucked right up along the side of the filter (as shown here). If you make a mistake, you can always either press Command-Z (PC: Ctrl-Z) to Undo your path and try again, or click-and-drag the little handles that appear on the path and use them to bend it (those are curve adjustment handles).

Step 13:

Now that bend is the hard part—the rest is simple. Once you release the mouse button, you just move the Pen tool cursor past the bottom right of the piece of cardboard, click once, and a straight line connects the two points. Basically you're going to draw a box made of paths around the area you want to select. When you get back to the original point you started with, a tiny little circle will appear at the bottom right of your Pen tool cursor (as seen here) telling you that you've come full circle. If you click on that original point, you'll have completed your path.

Step 14:

Once you've completed your path, you can turn your path into a selection (as shown here, which was our goal all along) by pressing Command-Return (PC: Ctrl-Enter). So, here's the thing: once you have a selection in place, you can't accidentally paint outside of it, so when you're cloning, you don't have to worry about accidentally cloning over part of the filter—you can't—you can only clone inside that selected area. I use this trick again and again to make my cloning life easier.

Step 15:

Press S to get the Clone Stamp tool (from the Toolbox) and choose a medium, soft-edged brush from the Brush Picker. Then press-and-hold the Option (PC: Alt) key and click once to the right of your selected area (as shown here) to sample a nearby area of background.

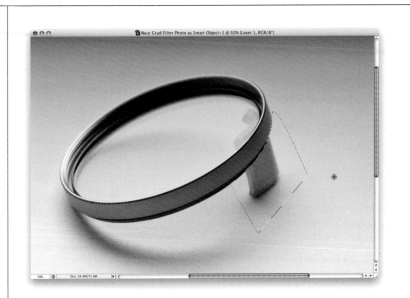

Step 16:

Now move your cursor over the piece of cardboard, and start painting (cloning) over it. As you do, it clones that area of background you sampled over the cardboard. Go ahead and keep painting until the piece of cardboard inside the selected area is gone (it's been cloned over. You'll want to keep sampling different background areas to match the tone and color). You can then Deselect by pressing Command-D (PC: Ctrl-D). Again, you have no worries of accidentally erasing or cloning over the filter itself—you can only clone inside the selected area.

Step 17:
Once the piece of cardboard on the outside of the filter has been cloned over (as seen here), it's time to work on the top of the cardboard, which appears inside the glass. The quickest way to select the inside of the glass is to use the Quick Selection tool, so press W to get it from the Toolbox. Just start painting a small stroke inside the glass area, and a second later, the inside oval of the filter is selected (this tool is pretty darn amazing).

Step 18:
Before we start cloning, just a quick reminder: we're still working on that flattened layer we created back in Step 10 (you can see it at the top of the layer stack). Okay, now onto the cloning. Switch back to the Clone Stamp tool and click it once inside your oval selection, but to the left of the cardboard piece you want to clone away (as shown here).

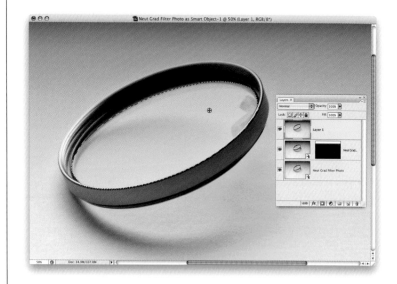

Step 19:
Now just clone right over the top of that cardboard piece until it's completely gone. Don't deselect yet, because we need that selection for our next step.

Step 20:
Although this is a neutral density gradient filter, you can't really see the gradation in the glass from dark to light (like you can when you hold it in your hand in person), but we can add that in Photoshop (okay, I basically had to add it in Photoshop since it didn't show up in the shot). At the bottom of the Layers panel, click on the Create a New Layer icon to create a new blank layer. Now, get the Gradient tool again, and click-and-drag a gradient from the right side of the filter diagonally down to the left bottom (as shown here).

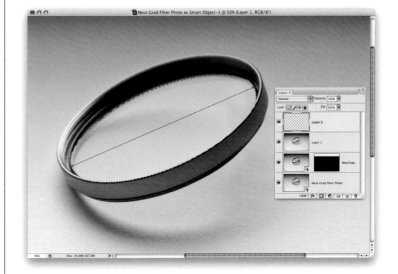

Step 21:

This fills the oval with a really fake look-ing black-to-transparent gradient, as seen here. You can now press Command-D (PC: Ctrl-D) to Deselect.

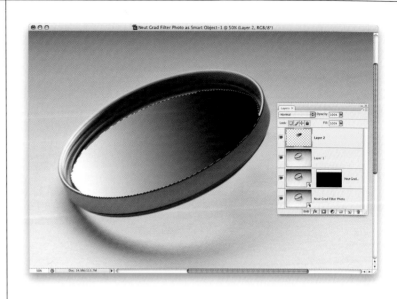

Step 22:

What makes the gradient look so fake is the fact that it's solid—it's not see-through like real glass. So, simply lower the Opacity setting of this gradient layer in the Layers panel until it looks see-through and more realistic (here I lowered the Opacity setting to around 39%). Now choose Flatten Image from the Layers panel's flyout menu to flatten your layers.

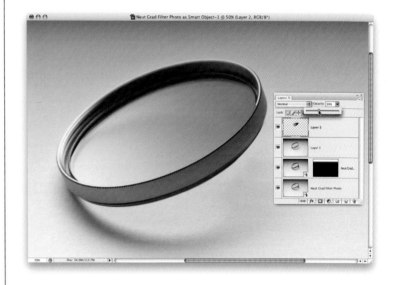

Step 23:

The final step (as always) is sharpening. I would apply some nice, punchy sharpening (after all, your subject is made of metal and glass), so go to your Actions panel and apply the Sharpen High action you created. In fact, you might even want to apply it a second time to really make it punchy. That completes the edits, and the before and after images are shown below.

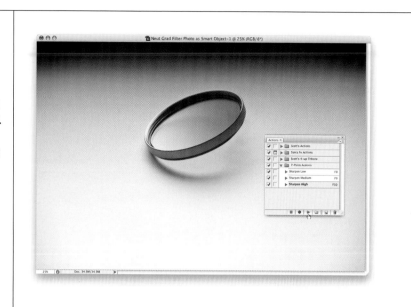

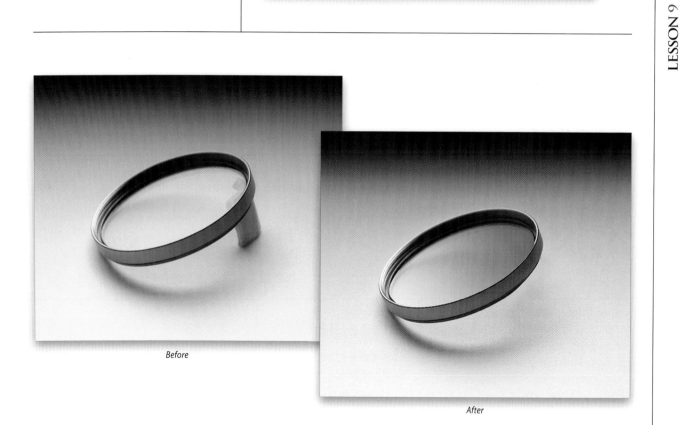

Before

After

LESSON 10

This was definitely a throwaway shot, taken at a small fishing village near Bar Harbor, Maine. I was waiting for my shooting buddy to catch up with me, so I cranked off this fairly lame shot of a porch. I knew it was lame when I took it, but once I saw it later in Photoshop, I thought the porch looked okay, but it was the detail in the shot that actually detracted from it. The solution? Make the porch a silhouette and try to make the sky look warmer and more like sunset. You can almost do this whole thing in Camera Raw itself. Well, almost.

LESSON 10

Step One:

Open the unadjusted photo in Camera Raw. This photo is a JPEG, so to open it within Camera Raw, you have to first go under the File menu and choose Open (PC: Open As). When you find the JPEG photo you want to open, click on it, but don't click Open yet. Instead, choose Camera Raw from the Format (PC: Open As) pop-up menu. Then click the Open button, and it opens in Camera Raw (as shown here).

Step Two:

This photo is pretty bland, so we're going to take some creative license and change the photo into more of a silhouette to give it some visual interest. We'll start by greatly warming up the photo by adjusting the white balance. If this had been a RAW photo, we could just choose the Shade preset from the White Balance pop-up menu, but since this is a JPEG (and the only available preset is Auto), we'll have to warm it up manually. Drag the Temperature slider way over to the right towards yellow to +60. Then drag the Tint slider over to the right, as well, to +11.

SCOTT KELBY

Step Three:

Now the color of the light is more like dusk, but the intensity of the light is too bright, so we're going to lower the exposure to make it more like dusk. This is an easy adjustment—just drag the Exposure slider to the left until it reads –1.80.

Step Four:

To give us the silhouette effect, you'll have to increase the blacks (shadows) by quite a bit. So, drag the Blacks slider over to the right until all the detail pretty much falls into the shadows. In this instance, drag over to around 41 and that should do the trick.

Step Five:

To pump up the intensity of the color, drag the Vibrance slider over to the right (I use Vibrance instead of Saturation, because Vibrance increases the least saturated colors most, and affects the already saturated colors the least). Here I dragged the Vibrance slider over to +45. Now go ahead and click the Open Image button to open the image in Photoshop.

Step Six:

Once it's open in Photoshop, we're going to darken the top of the sky (kind of a neutral density gradient filter effect). Press D to set your Foreground color to black, then click on the Create New Adjustment Layer icon at the bottom of the Layers panel, and choose Gradient from the pop-up menu (as shown here).

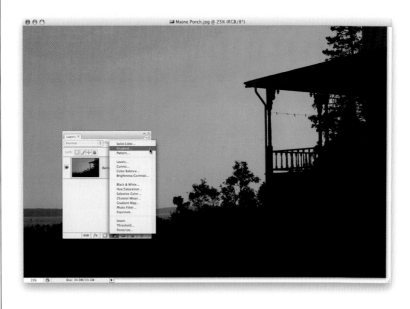

Step Seven:

When the Gradient Fill dialog appears, the gradient darkens the ground instead of the sky (that's the default setting), so you'll need to turn on the Reverse checkbox (shown circled here), but don't click OK yet.

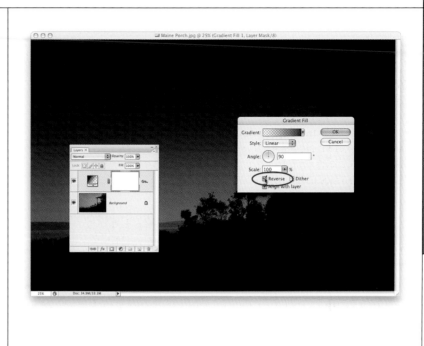

Step Eight:

Also in the Gradient Fill dialog, click once directly on the gradient thumbnail itself to bring up the Gradient Editor. You control how far down your gradient extends by clicking-and-dragging the top-right opacity stop to the left (as shown here). Now, here's the weird thing: you don't get a live preview as you drag this stop—you have to drag it over to the left and release the mouse button to see the results (I have no idea why it's this way). So, click-and-drag it over to the left a little so the gradient doesn't extend all the way to the bottom, and the gradient is mostly in the sky. Okay, now you can click OK in both dialogs.

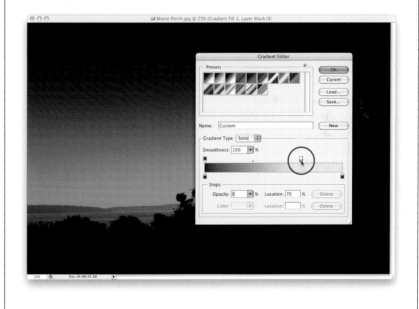

Step Nine:

To have your gradient blend in with your color photo (instead of covering it), change the blend mode of this Gradient layer to Soft Light (as shown here). Then flatten your layers by clicking on the triangle in the top right of the Layers panel and choosing Flatten Image from the panel's flyout menu.

Step 10:

To increase the contrast and add more punch to the color, we're going to do a Lab color move. Go under the Image menu, under Mode, and choose Lab Color. Now, go under the Image menu and choose Apply Image. The only thing you have to do in this dialog is to change the Blending pop-up menu to Soft Light. That does the trick. Click OK, and then go back under the Image menu, under Mode, and choose RGB Color.

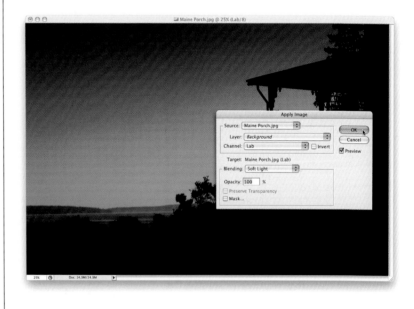

Step 11:

To finish this project off, let's wrap it up with some good, old-fashioned sharpening. Go to the Actions panel, click on your Sharpen High action, and then click on the Play Selection icon (as shown here). The before and after images are shown below.

Before

After

LESSON 11

This was actually taken behind that church in Santa Fe you saw earlier, and the colors looked really nice and vibrant—until I opened the photo in Photoshop. This is one of those images where you have to double-process it, making two versions of the same photo, and then put parts of each together to make one image that's the best of the two. This one takes a few more steps, but the final image is worth it (because the original image would never have seen the light of day).

LESSON 11

Step One:
Open the unadjusted RAW photo in Camera Raw (as shown here).

SCOTT KELBY

Step Two:
Let's warm up that yellow wall by dragging the White Balance Temperature slider over to the right, towards yellow, stopping at 7700.

Step Three:

Now let's fix the overall exposure, starting with the highlights. Drag the Exposure slider over to the right to around +0.60, which makes the overall photo brighter, but take a peek up in the histogram. Part of the histogram must be touching the right wall, because the highlight clipping warning triangle (which appears in the upper-right corner of the histogram) has turned solid red. An easy fix.

Step Four:

To stop that clipping in the Red channel, just drag the Recovery slider over to the right until the clipping warning goes away (you'll only have to drag over to around 3).

Step Five:

To make our yellow color more saturated (and have the photo look less washed out), let's increase the shadows. Drag the Blacks slider to the right to around 18 (as shown here). Hey, we're starting to get there—it's looking pretty decent (well, as long as you don't look at the windows, but that's something we'll fix shortly).

Step Six:

Now let's add some snap to the midtones by adding clarity (which, again, you can think of as midtone sharpening). First (and as always), before you add clarity, double-click on the Zoom tool (the magnifying glass icon) to jump to a 100% view. Now, drag the Clarity slider over to around 33.

Step Seven:

To give the whole photo a color boost, head down to the Vibrance slider and drag it over to the right a bit (to around +14) to make the colors a bit more vibrant. Doing this did make the highlights clip just a little bit (I saw the warning go off up in the histogram), so I dragged the Recovery slider from 3 to 5 and that cured it (so do the same, ya know, if losing critical detail in your highlights is a concern to you). Now, press-and-hold the Shift key and you'll see that the Open Image button has changed to Open Object. Click that button to open this photo as a Smart Object in Photoshop.

Step Eight:

Here's the photo opened in Photoshop as a Smart Object (you can tell it's a Smart Object by the tiny icon in the layer thumbnail's bottom-right corner). Next we need to fix those windows (add some of the blue from the sky into them, and replace that yellow color cast). So, we need to duplicate this layer without it being tied to the original Smart Object. To do that, Control-click (PC: Right-click) on the layer, and from the contextual menu that appears, choose New Smart Object via Copy.

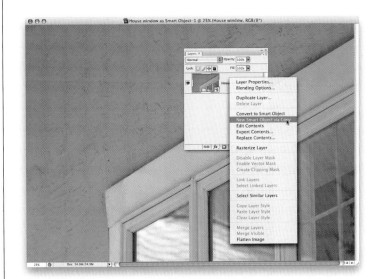

Step Nine:

Here's the duplicate layer in the Layers panel. We need to reprocess just this duplicate layer back in Camera Raw, so double-click directly on the layer's thumbnail (as shown here).

Step 10:

To add some blue reflection (from the sky) into the windows, we're going to make two white balance moves: (1) choose Fluorescent from the White Balance pop-up menu to add lots of blue into the image (but it looks more like a purplish blue in this particular photo), and then (2) to get rid of the purplish look, drag the Tint slider to 0. That's it—two simple white balance changes. Now you can click OK.

Step 11:

When you click OK, your changes are automatically updated in your layered document (you can see the more blue layer in the Layers panel). Now, although we like the windows being blue, we don't like the blue window molding, and the blue has affected our nice, punchy, once-yellow wall, as well, so it's time for some simple layer masking. Click on the Add Layer Mask icon at the bottom of the Layers panel.

Step 12:

You need to put a selection around everything but the window area, and since this selection is made up of nothing but straight lines, the easiest tool to use is probably the Polygonal Lasso tool, or if you're comfortable with the Pen tool, it works great, too. (*Tip:* Try selecting this wall using the Quick Selection tool [W]—just click-and-paint a quick stroke or two and the wall is selected for you!) To use the Polygonal Lasso tool (press Shift-L until you have it), it's pretty much a connect-the-dot tool: you click once, move your cursor to the next point, and a line appears as you drag. So, you just click-and-move your way around your image, and each time you a click, a straight selection line is drawn between your points. When you get back to where you started, click on the first point you created, and it completes the selection. So, get started—start clicking-and-moving your cursor around everything but the window to select it (as shown here).

Step 13:

Once the wall is selected, make sure your Foreground color is set to black, and then press Option-Delete (PC: Alt-Backspace) to fill your selected area's mask with black, which reveals the original yellow wall from the layer below it. Don't deselect quite yet.

Step 14:

Now you need to select the window only (the opposite of what you had selected), so while your selection is still in place, go under the Select menu and choose Inverse to invert your selection and select everything but the wall (giving you a selection of the windows). If you mess this up, don't sweat it—just deselect, then use the Polygonal Lasso tool to select the entire window area (so it looks like the selection you see here).

Step 15:

In the Layers panel, click directly on the blue layer's image thumbnail (as shown here) to select the photo rather than its layer mask where we've been working. You haven't deselected yet, so press Command-J (PC: Ctrl-J) to take the selected area (the bluish windows) and put them up on their own separate layer.

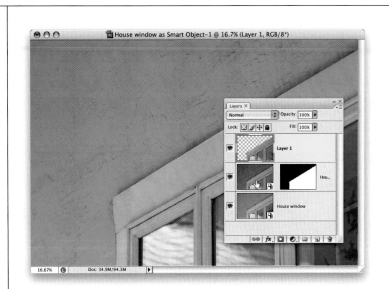

Step 16:

Now, we want to remove the blue from the window frame, but there's more than blue there—there's also some red (you can see it in the frame if you look closely), so we'll need to remove both to get to a solid white frame. Go under the Image menu, under Adjustments, and choose Hue/Saturation. From the Edit pop-up menu at the top, choose Blues, then drag the Saturation amount to –100 to remove the blue in the window and window frame. Don't click OK quite yet.

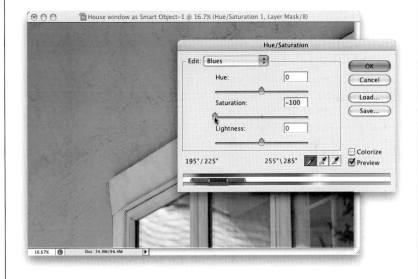

LESSON 11

Step 17:

Now choose Reds from the Edit pop-up menu, and then lower the Saturation amount of the Reds to –100, as well (which removes the red from the window and window frame, and now they're pretty much white). Now you can click OK.

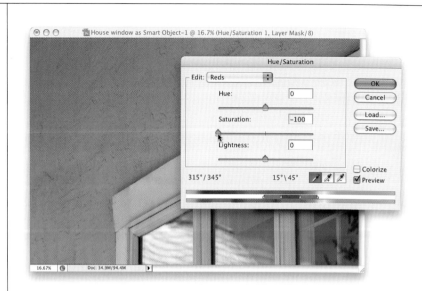

Step 18:

So, we accomplished one goal—getting rid of the blue and red color casts in the window frame—but we also lost all the blue in the glass window itself (which we didn't want to do), so we're going to knock out the window on our top layer, to reveal just the blue window on the layer below. Start by adding a layer mask to this top layer (click on the Add Layer Mask icon at the bottom of the Layers panel), then get either the Polygonal Lasso tool or the Quick Selection tool, and put a selection around the windowpane on the left (as shown here).

Step 19:
Once your selection is in place, press Option-Delete (PC: Alt-Backspace) to fill that selected area in the mask with black. This reveals the bluer layer directly below it, making that windowpane nice and blue (as seen here).

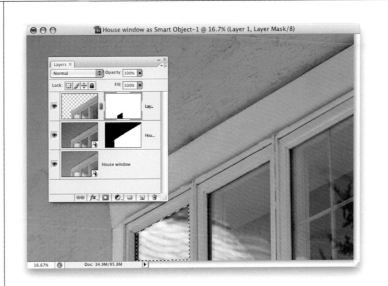

Step 20:
Now, select the center pane and do the same thing—fill it with black to reveal the layer below it.

Step 21:

Of course, do the same thing with the third windowpane (select it and fill it with black), so the blue shows through (as seen here, where all three windowpanes have been masked). Press Command-D (PC: Ctrl-D) to Deselect.

Step 22:

Now that we've come this far, and we can see what is nearly the final image, the blue looks a little overwhelming, so click on the center layer (the blue layer), then lower the Opacity setting until it looks more natural (in this case, I lowered the opacity to 80%).

Step 23:

Now it's time to flatten the layers (in the Layers panel's flyout menu) and then run your sharpening action (I chose Sharpen High in my Actions panel, as shown here) to complete the edit. A before and after are shown below.

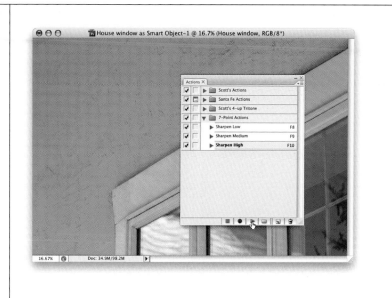

Before

After

LESSON 12

This was taken by my buddy, Dave, and he asked me to see what I could do with it. As it turned out, the final version of this photo is the inspiration for this book (this is the image I showed my brother that he thought looked like a Kinkade. Then I showed him the original, and he asked me to show him exactly how I got to the final image. Once I did, he said, "You should write a book that starts with a 'crappy' image and takes you all the way through the process to the final image." You're halfway through that book now). By the way, this shot was taken in L.A. I kid you not.

Step One:

Open the unadjusted original photo in Camera Raw. This image was taken as a JPEG, so to open it in Camera Raw, go under the File menu and choose Open (PC: Open As). When you find the JPEG file you want to open, click on it, then choose Camera Raw from the Format (PC: Open As) pop-up menu, and click Open. This opens the JPEG image in Camera Raw.

DAVE MOSER

Step Two:

Start by adjusting the white balance. In this case, we're going to make a creative decision with our white balance to make the photo much warmer, and less green and murky. To do that, drag the Temperature slider to the right, towards yellow, until it reads +44. This gives the overall photo a warmer feel (but it still looks very washed out).

Step Three:

To get rid of the washed out look and bring some saturation to our colors, we'll need to increase the shadows. Drag the Blacks slider to the right until the colors look vivid and saturated (in this example, I dragged over to 15).

Step Four:

Now, the side of the boat house is looking quite dark after increasing the Blacks amount, so drag the Fill Light slider to the right a little bit to open up some of those midtone shadow areas (as shown here, where I dragged the Fill Light slider to 10).

Step Five:

This shot was taken late in the day, so the sun is lower in the sky, but the sunlight that's beaming in is very bright. To take the edge off that light, decrease the very brightest highlights in the photo by dragging the Recovery slider quite a bit to the right (as shown here, where I dragged it to 40). This really "clamps down" on those highlights, and this is a trick I use quite often to fix a very bright sky, even if there's no clipping of highlights in the sky.

Step Six:

Now we're going to increase the overall exposure a little bit (it didn't look like we were going to need to do this at first, but once we increased the shadows and recovered the extreme highlights, it just looks like it needs to be a little bit brighter overall). Drag the Exposure slider to the right just a little bit (over to +0.55) to add a little brightness.

Step Seven:

The last thing we'll do here in Camera Raw is to add some nice contrast in the Tone Curve panel. Click on the second icon from the left at the top of the panel area, and when the Tone Curve panel appears, click on the Point tab. From the Curve pop-up menu, choose Medium Contrast to make the shadows a bit darker and the highlights a bit brighter (basically adding some nice contrast). Now, press-and-hold the Shift key and the Open Image button will change into the Open Object button. Click that button to open this processed JPEG as a Smart Object in Photoshop.

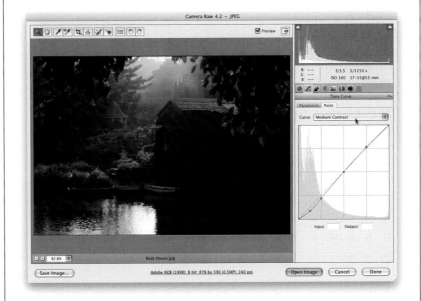

Step Eight:

The image opens in Photoshop as a Smart Object, but we're going to need to double-process this photo to bring some more natural colors back. So, Control-click (PC: Right-click) near the Smart Object layer's name to bring up a contextual menu, and from that menu, choose New Smart Object via Copy. This duplicates the Smart Object layer, but the duplicate will not be tied to the original Smart Object like it would have been if you had just duplicated the layer as if it were a regular layer.

Step Nine:

Once your duplicate Smart Object layer appears, go to the Layers panel and double-click directly on its thumbnail to open it in Camera Raw. When it opens, the settings you last used are still in place, but what we want to do is create a less yellow version. To do that, you just have to do two things: (1) in the White Balance pop-up menu, change the white balance to Auto, and then (2) increase the Exposure setting quite a bit (to +1.80, as shown here). That's it—just those two changes and we have a totally different look. Now click OK to have those changes applied to your duplicate Smart Object layer back in Photoshop.

Step 10:

Once your duplicate Smart Object layer is updated with your new white balance and exposure changes, press-and-hold the Option (PC: Alt) key and click on the Add Layer Mask icon at the bottom of the Layers panel (as shown here) to hide this brighter, bluer layer behind a black layer mask. All you'll see now is the original image from the bottom layer.

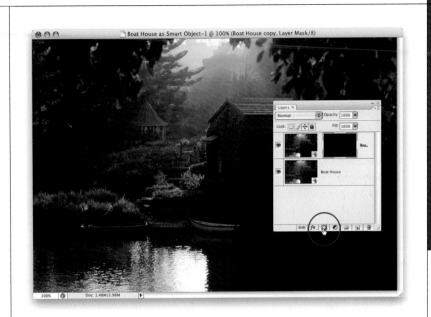

Step 11:

Now we're going to reveal some part of the duplicate layer. With your Foreground color set to white, press B to get the Brush tool. Click on the brush thumbnail in the Options Bar and choose a very large, soft-edged brush (around the size you see here) from the Brush Picker.

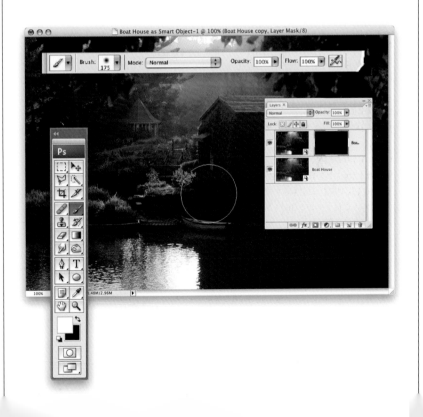

Step 12:

Start painting over the boathouse, steps, gazebo, plants, grass, and pretty much everything in the center area of the photo, but stay away from the edges of the photo—the water, and the sky. Focus on just the area in the center of the photo and the boathouse. As you paint, the cooler version is revealed from that duplicate layer.

Step 13:

Continue painting until the entire boathouse, surrounding grass, steps, etc., are fully painted in (as seen here).

Step 14:

If the area you painted in seems too intense (it does seem a bit intense to me), then go to the Layers panel and lower the Opacity setting of this top layer (here I lowered it to 80%, and I thought it looked much better—taking the edge off the color just a little bit). Now you can flatten the image if you like (but it's not necessary).

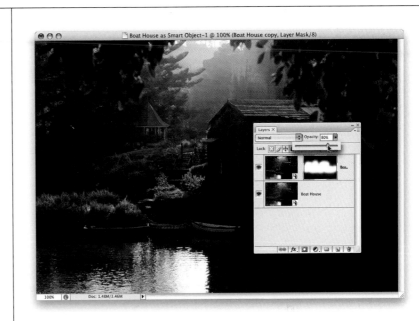

Step 15:

To really make the colors pop in this image, we're going to use the Lab color move. Start by going under the Image menu, under Mode, and choose Lab Color. Then go under the Image menu again, but this time choose Apply Image. When the Apply Image dialog appears, change the Blending pop-up menu to Soft Light, then see which of the three channels (Lab, "a," or "b") looks best blended like this (in the Channel pop-up menu). Personally, I think the "b" channel looks great here, because it makes the photo warmer and the rest of the color more intense. However, since they're so intense, you might want to back off the intensity just a bit by lowering the Opacity setting to 80%, as shown here, and then click OK.

Step 16:

Go back under the Image menu, under Mode, and choose RGB Color to change the color mode back to RGB. Now let's deal with that lame-looking water. If you were thinking, "Boy, this would have looked a lot better if that water were still and glassy," then this photo is about to look a lot better. Press M to get the Rectangular Marquee tool, and make a large rectangular selection from the top of the image down to where the bottom of the selection runs right along the bottom of the boats.

Step 17:

Press Command-J (PC: Ctrl-J) to put that selected area up on its own separate layer (you can see this layer in the Layers panel). Now, press Command-T (PC: Ctrl-T) to bring up the Free Transform bounding box around your layer. Then you'll need to Control-click (PC: Right-click) anywhere inside that bounding box, and a contextual menu of possible transformations will appear. Choose Flip Vertical (as shown here).

Step 18:
This flips your current layer upside down (as seen here). Press the Return (PC: Enter) key to lock in your transformation. Now, you're going to use this flipped layer to create your still, glassy water look.

Step 19:
Press V to get the Move tool, press-and-hold the Shift key (to keep your layers aligned), and click-and-drag your flipped layer straight downward until the top of it touches the bottom of your original image's boats, creating the still, glassy reflection you see here. This looks much, much better, but there is a problem—the shoreline of the lake bank isn't straight, and some of it is cut off by your flipped reflection. It may be a little hard to see here at this small size in the book, but onscreen (or in print) it would be really obvious, so we have to fix it.

Step 20:

Go to the Layers panel, and click on the Eye icon to the left of the top layer's thumbnail to hide the layer (so you can clearly see the lake bank). Click on the Background layer to activate it and then press L to get the Lasso tool. Click-and-drag to slowly trace right along the edge of the lake bank, on the right side of the image, where it meets the water. Then press-and-hold the Option (PC: Alt) key, release your mouse button, and click once, which turns your regular freeform Lasso tool into the Polygonal Lasso tool. Now you can drag straight-line selections with it—so box in the area right above the lake bank (as shown here).

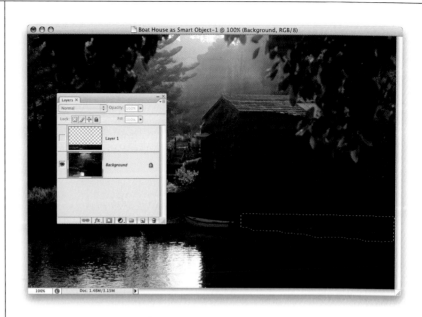

Step 21:

Click to the left of the top layer's thumb-nail in the Layers panel to make it visible again, and then click on the layer to make it active. Your selection will still be in place (from the lake bank on the lower layer), so now press Delete (PC: Backspace) to delete the overlapping area from your top layer. *Note:* If the edge of the deleted area looks harsh and jaggy, press Command-Z (PC: Ctrl-Z) to Undo the delete, and add a 2-pixel feather to the selected area first (by going under the Select menu, under Modify, and choosing Feather), then hit Delete. This feathering softens the edges and helps avoid that harsh, jaggy edge. I doubt you'll need this feathering in this instance, but hey—ya never know. Press Command-D (PC: Ctrl-D) to Deselect.

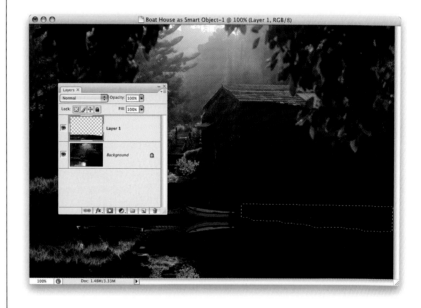

Step 22:

Now we're going to "burn in" the edges of the photo, so it looks like a soft light is shining on the center. Start by choosing Flatten Image from the Layers panel's flyout menu to flatten the layers. Once they're flattened, click-and-drag the Background layer onto the Create a New Layer icon at the bottom of the Layers panel to duplicate it, and then change the blend mode of this duplicate layer to Multiply (as shown here). This makes the image twice as dark.

Step 23:

Press M to get the Rectangular Marquee tool and draw a selection that is inset approximately 1" from the border of your image (as shown here). Now, to greatly soften the edges of your selection, go under the Select menu, under Modify, and choose Feather. When the Feather Selection dialog appears, enter 100 pixels (for this smaller, low-resolution photo) or 200 for a standard, high-res digital camera photo. Click OK.

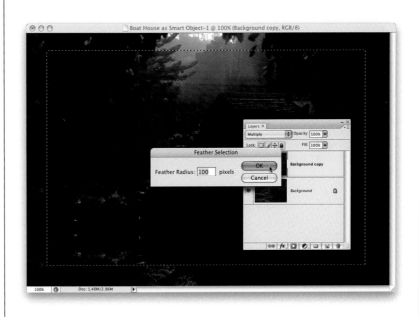

Step 24:

Now press the Delete (PC: Backspace) key to knock a very soft-edged hole out of your darker layer, revealing your lighter layer beneath it (as shown here). This leaves the edges of your photo darkened, and a soft light effect on the center of your photo. Now you can deselect by pressing Command-D (PC: Ctrl-D), then you can flatten the layers by choosing Flatten Image from the Layers panel's flyout menu.

Step 25:

The final step is to sharpen the photo, so open your Actions panel (found under the Window menu). Since this photo is of a softer nature, click on the Sharpen Medium action and then click on the Play Selection icon to apply your sharpening. The before and after images are shown on the next page.

Before

After

LESSON 13

This image has such a big problem that after using The System, I still had to cheat and borrow a sky from another shot taken in the same location about 30 minutes later. I generally don't like to composite two images like this, but if really desperate (like I was here), I will do it, even though it feels a little like cheating to me (even though I took both shots myself, and they're both taken in the same location during the same shoot). But, if you wind up in a similar situation, at least you'll know what to do, eh?

LESSON 13

Step One:
Open the unadjusted original RAW photo in Camera Raw. This image was taken before dusk with a long exposure to get the water to look silky, but it also totally blew out the sky (and the sky wasn't so great to begin with). So, the rocks are okay (a little dark), and we can work with the water. The color needs work too, but that's easy enough.

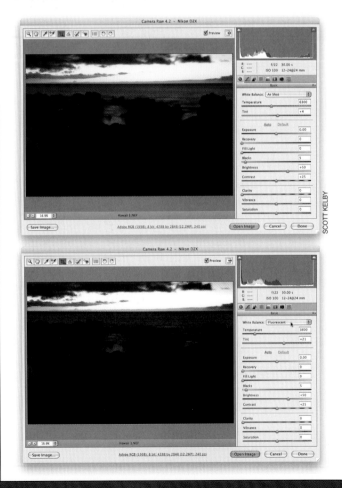

SCOTT KELBY

Step Two:
First let's choose a white balance that looks better. Since this is a RAW photo, we can just choose a preset from the White Balance pop-up menu, so choose Fluorescent (as shown here).

Step Three:

The default Camera Raw setting has the shadows (Blacks) set to 5, which makes the rocks almost solid black, so drag the Blacks slider back to the left to 0, which brings some of the detail in the rocks back. Then, to get a little more light on those rocks, drag the Fill Light slider to the right and open up that area a bit (here I dragged the Fill Light slider over to 20).

Step Four:

Let's open the midtones a bit (again, to try and keep as much light on those rocks as you can, because later we're going to wind up darkening them as a result of adjusting something else). So, drag the Brightness slider over to the right (as shown here, where I dragged it over to +58).

Step Five:

When you click the Open Image button, the image opens in Photoshop. The rocks look okay (not great, just okay), but the sky is a mess. This is one of those shots where we lost so much detail in the camera that we can't bring that detail back in Camera Raw. If you had just clipped the highlights a little bit, and you shot in RAW mode, a lot of times you can recover those lost highlights, but when they're this gone, you have to go to plan B. In this case, plan B is to use a different sky. I took a photo from approximately the same position, but about 30 minutes later, just after the sun had gone down (so I didn't have to worry as much about blowing out the highlights), and I got the bonus of some much nicer clouds that moved into position.

Step Six:

Open the second RAW photo (as shown here), and to make sure the colors match the first image, set the white balance the same (choose Fluorescent from the White Balance pop-up menu). If you look up in the histogram, you can see that the highlight clipping warning is on, so we'll have to work on that.

SCOTT KELBY

Step Seven:

Luckily, there's not nearly the problem with the highlights in this sky as in the previous photo, so we can probably fix it pretty easily. Start by lowering the Exposure setting a bit (down to –0.45), and then increase the Recovery amount to 55, which kind of clamps down the sky a bit. If you look at the histogram now, you'll see the clipping warning is off and we have detail in all of the sky (even in the brightest parts).

Step Eight:

A bigger problem than that tiny bit of highlight clipping is the fact that the horizon isn't straight (apparently, I was trying to see just how many things I could do wrong on this shoot). Get the Straighten tool (A) from the toolbar at the top (it's next to the Crop tool), and drag it right along the horizon line (I dragged from left to right, as shown here).

Step Nine:

When you release the mouse button, the Straighten tool applies the exact amount of rotation necessary to perfectly straighten the photo. So, when you open the photo in Photoshop, it will open straightened. Go ahead and click the Open Image button.

Step 10:

Now you have two photos open in Photoshop: one with nice silky water and brighter rocks, and one with a good sky. Any chance of these two getting together? I bet they'd make a lovely child.

Step 11:
Get the Move tool (V), press-and-hold the Shift key, and drag the "good rocks" photo on top of the "good sky" photo (it appears on its own separate layer, as shown here). By the way, the reason you press-and-hold the Shift key before you drag is so when you drag the photo on top, it aligns itself to fit perfectly centered within the document. Otherwise, the photo lands where you release the mouse button.

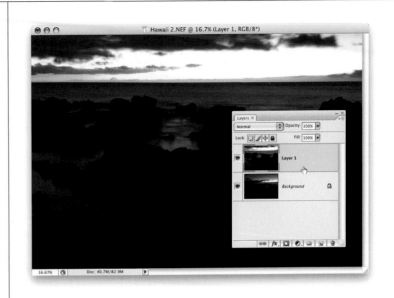

Step 12:
We need to align the two horizon lines (which are off by quite a bit), so go to the Layers panel and lower the Opacity setting of the top layer (Layer 1) to around 40%. Now you can clearly see through this layer to the horizon line in the photo on the Background layer.

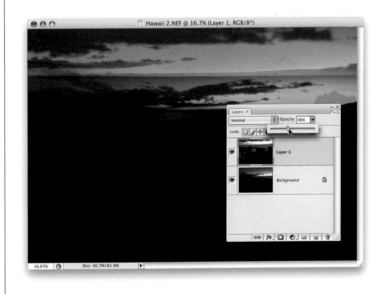

Step 13:

Press-and-hold the Shift key, take the Move tool, and click-and-drag straight downward (holding down the Shift key as you drag will keep it perfectly straight). Drag down until the two horizon lines are perfectly aligned (as shown here). Then you can raise the Opacity setting of the top layer back to 100%.

Step 14:

Now we'll use a layer mask to blend the two photos together (so click on the Add Layer Mask icon at the bottom of the Layers panel), but we're not going to use the Brush tool to paint away the old sky on the top layer. Instead, we're going to make a rectangular selection of everything from the horizon line up (using the Rectangular Marquee tool [M], as shown here).

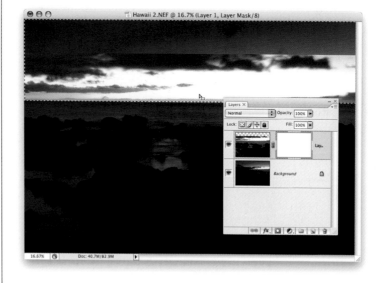

Step 15:

You want the transition between the good rocks and the new sky to be smooth, so let's feather (soften) the edges a bit. Go under the Select menu, under Modify, and choose Feather. When the Feather Selection dialog appears, enter 5 as your Feather Radius, and click OK.

Step 16:

To remove the old sky, make sure your Foreground color is set to black, then press Option-Delete (PC: Alt-Backspace) to fill the selected area of your mask with black. This hides the old sky from the good rocks photo.

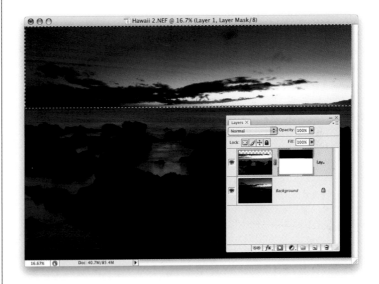

Step 17:

Now you can deselect by pressing Command-D (PC: Ctrl-D), and the two images are blended together seamlessly. Next, we're going to punch up the colors, so go under the Image menu, under Mode, and choose Lab Color. When the warning dialog comes up, go ahead and click Flatten.

Step 18:

Now that you're in Lab color mode, go under the Image menu and choose Apply Image. When the Apply Image dialog appears, set the Blending pop-up menu to Soft Light, then try all three of the channels (from the Channel pop-up menu), including Lab, "a," and "b." In this case, I think the Lab channel looks the best of the three, but it's a bit too intense, and too punchy. Luckily, there's an "amount of punch" control—it's the Opacity setting. Lower the Opacity setting to 50%, and it looks much better—you get the added contrast and punch, without the photo becoming too saturated. Click OK to close the dialog, then go back under the Image menu, under Mode, and switch back to RGB Color.

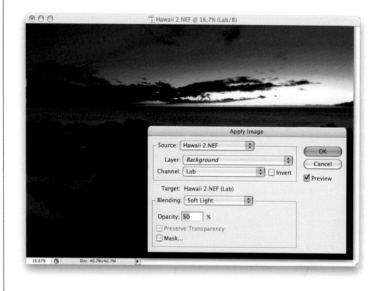

Step 19:

This Apply Image Lab color move is what I was talking about earlier in Step Four when I said something we're going to do later on is going to make our rocks darker (which is what happened here). We can use one of our seven points to help us out. Start by pressing Command-J (PC: Ctrl-J) to duplicate the Background layer, then go under the Filter menu and choose Convert to Smart Filters.

Step 20:

Once you've converted the duplicate layer for Smart Filters, go under the Image menu, under Adjustments, and choose Shadow/Highlight (just about everything else is grayed out). When the dialog appears, lower the Shadows Amount to only 20%, as shown here, to open those rocks back up a bit, then click OK.

Step 21:

The Shadow/Highlight control opened up all the shadows on the entire layer (and this is already a fairly dark image), but we only want them opened up a bit on the rocks. That's no problem, because we converted our duplicate layer for Smart Filters (which adds a layer mask to our filtered layer). Click directly on the white layer mask, and then press Command-I (PC: Ctrl-I), which inverts the mask (as seen here) and hides the version with the opened-up shadows behind that black mask.

Step 22:

Now you're going to paint over the rocks and reveal the lighter version of them, while leaving the rest of the photo untouched. Set your Foreground color to white, get the Brush tool (B), choose a medium-sized, soft-edged brush from the Brush Picker, and start painting over the rocks (as shown here). As you paint, they become lighter. Now you can choose Flatten Image from the Layers panel's flyout menu to flatten the layers.

Step 23:

The last step, of course, is to sharpen the final image, so go to the Actions panel and apply the Sharpen Medium action you created back in Lesson 1. The before and after images are shown below.

Before

After

LESSON 14

If this background looks familiar, it should. It was taken at the same time and place as my shot of Matt earlier, but my problem isn't the background this time, it's getting the color cast off the camera and my buddy (and *Photoshop User TV* co-host) Dave Cross's shirt. We can do some of the work in Camera Raw, but since the focus of the shot is the camera, we can pull a few Photoshop layer mask and sharpening tricks to make it really stand out, make it really sharp, and make the overall image really pop. The Clarity feature really does a wonderful job here, too.

LESSON 14

Step One:
Open the unadjusted original RAW photo in Camera Raw.

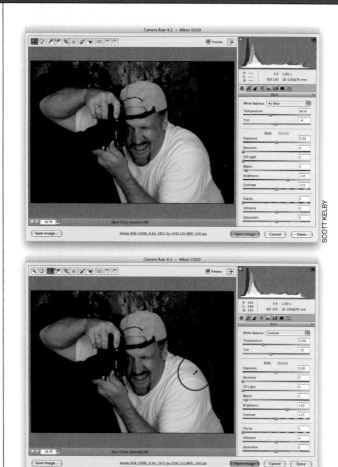

SCOTT KELBY

Step Two:
Since there's an area on Dave's shirt that looks like it should be light gray, you can just grab the White Balance tool (I) from the toolbar and click it once on a light gray area (as shown here, circled in red). This removes some of the yellow cast caused by the background Dave's posed in front of. Light reflects whatever color it hits, so Dave, his clothes, camera, etc., would all have a yellowish/reddish tint. If you look at his shirt in Step One, then compare his shirt here, you can see the shirt has much less of a yellow color cast now.

Step Three:

We want the camera to really be clear and crisp in this photo (after all, it's a shot of Dave shooting), so increase the Exposure amount just a bit (I dragged the slider to +0.40) and then drag the Fill Light slider to the right (to 25) to open up some of the dark areas on the camera itself (everything else in the photo is already light enough, but the camera could be brighter, and will suffer a little more in the next step when we balance out the shadows).

Step Four:

To bring back our color saturation and enhance the shadow areas, drag the Blacks slider to the right, as shown here, where I increased the amount to 19.

Step Five:

To add some extra sharpness and punch to the camera, increase the Clarity amount (here, I dragged over to 36) to really make that camera snap (I just set myself up with an opportunity to make a really lame camera/snap pun. I'm going to let this one slip by, but I want you to know, it isn't easy).

Step Six:

Now that we've made all these adjustments, Dave's starting to look a bit yellowish again (I like skin tones to be warm, but he's looking jaundiced). To cool Dave down a bit (wait for it… wait for it…), we'll just drag the White Balance Temperature slider over to the left a little bit, toward blue (I dragged to 4400), which helps take some of the excess yellow out. Now you can click the Open Image button to open this RAW image in Photoshop.

Step Seven:

Let's add some punch and contrast to the overall image using the Lab color move. Go under the Image menu, under Mode, and choose Lab Color. Then, go under the Image menu, and choose Apply Image. Change the Blending pop-up menu to Soft Light (you've probably noticed that I nearly always choose Soft Light as my blend mode here. It seems to work best for most situations, but if I run across an image where I really need the colors to pop even more, I switch the blend mode to Overlay. Those are the only two Apply Image blend modes I use). Of the three channels you can choose from the Channel pop-up menu (Lab, "a," or "b"), Lab looks best, but it's also too intense, so lower the Opacity setting to around 40%, and click OK. Now go back under the Image menu, under Mode, and choose RGB Color.

Step Eight:

Our problem now is that the camera body and lens are reflecting all those colors behind Dave (which is totally realistic—I just don't like the way it makes the camera look. I want it nice and black like it came off the showroom floor). A quick way to do this is to remove the color from the whole photo, and then just selectively paint a black-and-white version of part of the camera back in. Here's how: First, click-and-drag your Background layer onto the Create a New Layer icon at the bottom of the Layers panel to duplicate the layer. Press D to set your Foreground color to black and your Background color to white. Then click on the Create New Adjustment Layer icon at the bottom of the Layers panel and choose Gradient Map. This brings up the Gradient Map dialog (shown here), and it makes the image black and white.

Step Nine:

Now, we only want the layer directly below the Gradient Map adjustment layer to be black and white, so click OK in the Gradient Map dialog, then press Command-E (PC: Ctrl-E) to merge this adjustment layer with the layer below it, making it one single black-and-white layer. Let's hide that black-and-white layer behind a black layer mask by pressing-and-holding the Option (PC: Alt) key and clicking on the Add Layer Mask icon at the bottom of the Layers panel (as shown here). Now your black-and-white image is hidden behind that black mask.

Step 10:

With your Foreground color set to white, press Z and click on the camera to zoom in on the image. Press B to get the Brush tool, and then click on the brush thumbnail in the Options Bar. Choose a small, soft-edged brush and start painting over the barrel of the lens, then the body of the lens—basically everything on the camera but two things: (1) any part of the camera that is in color (like the gold letters on the lens, or the red VR symbol, etc.), and (2) the glass part of the lens itself (that way, we can leave some of the color reflecting in the glass).

Step 11:
Here you can see what it looks like when you've painted over most of the camera, but have avoided those parts of the lens that are supposed to be in color. So, how can you easily tell if you've really painted over all of the camera and lens areas? That little trick is in the next step.

Step 12:
To see just the mask itself, press-and-hold the Option (PC: Alt) key and click directly on the top layer's layer mask thumbnail. This gives you a view of just the mask (as shown here) and you can easily see the little areas you missed on the barrel and the camera itself. The first gap on the left is the glass part of the lens. The second gap, about two-thirds of the way up the barrel (right before where the camera body would start), is the gold lettering on the lens. Both of these gaps should be there, but all those other little black areas on the barrel of the lens are just areas I missed.

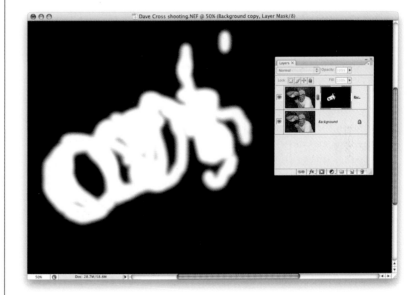

Step 13:

Take your Brush tool and paint directly on this mask (in white, of course), painting over any of those little areas you might have missed. I use this clean-up trick on just about every layer mask I create, because it's the only reliable way to see if you've really revealed everything evenly. Once you're done cleaning up your mask, do this: (1) click on the layer thumbnail for the Background copy layer, then (2) click back on the layer mask thumbnail to its right (don't Option-click, just click on it). That returns you to the full-color photo—if you started painting before you clicked back on the layer mask thumbnail, you'd be actually painting on the photo itself. When you click on the layer mask thumbnail, while you can still see the full-color photo, you're now painting on the mask.

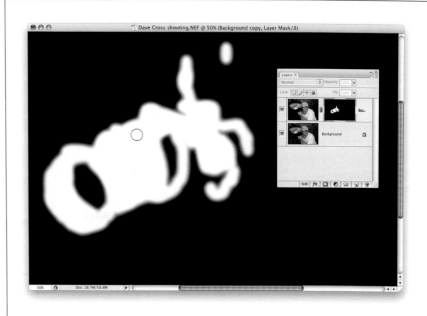

Step 14:

Now that you're back on the Background copy layer's mask, you can change anything you'd like (revealing more or less of the black-and-white camera), but once you're done, flatten the layers from the Layers panel's flyout menu. When you now look at the image, you might think that his shirt and hat are a little too bright and don't have as much detail as you'd like (well, at least that's what I thought). If that's the case (and you need to let that be the case for this step), click on the Create New Adjustment Layer icon at the bottom of the Layers panel and choose Curves. When the Curves dialog appears, click once on the center of the curve line and drag straight downward, which darkens the midtones in the entire image, and click OK.

Step 15:

Now the whole photo has darker mid-tones, but we only wanted to tweak his shirt and ballcap. That's no problem because we used an adjustment layer, which comes with its own built-in layer mask. First, press Command-I (PC: Ctrl-I) to Invert the mask, so the darkened mid-tones adjustment is hidden behind a black mask. Now, get the Brush tool, and with your Foreground color set to white, start painting over his ball cap (as shown here), which reveals the darker version as you paint.

Step 16:

Once his ball cap is painted in, then paint over the areas of his shirt that you felt were too bright, or were lacking detail. As you paint, make sure you don't turn his shirt gray. So, as you paint over an area, if it looks too gray, either press Command-Z (PC: Ctrl-Z) to undo your last paint stroke, or just press X to switch your Foreground color to black and paint over the too-gray area to hide it back behind the black mask. *Note:* I always start with the layer opacity set at 100%, so I can more clearly see the effect as I paint, then I go back and lower the opacity to where it looks right (and realistic) in the photo I'm adjusting. So, go to the Layers panel and lower the opacity of this Curves adjustment layer to around 70% (or to wherever it looks good to you), then flatten the layers.

Step 17:

Now step back, look at the photo, and ask yourself that critical Photoshop question we always ask ourselves, "What do I wish were different in this image?" Personally, I would like to see the camera a bit brighter, because after all of our adjustments, it still looks a little dark to me. So, we'll do that using a Shadow/Highlight adjustment. By now you know the drill: press Command-J (PC: Ctrl-J) to duplicate the Background layer, then go up to the Filter menu and choose Convert for Smart Filters.

Step 18:

Go under the Image menu, under Adjustments, and choose Shadow/Highlight. When the dialog appears, the default Shadows setting usually looks too bright, so lower the Shadows Amount to around 30% (or to wherever you think it looks good). Remember when using this feature, don't worry about how the rest of the photo looks—just focus on how the area you want to adjust looks, and in this case, at about 30% the camera looks much better. So, click OK and we'll worry about the rest of the photo in the next step.

Step 19:

The reason we went through that whole Convert for Smart Filters thing is so we could have a layer mask added to our adjustment (as seen here). Click on the Smart Filters layer mask thumbnail that's added below your duplicate layer (that's where the Smart Filters thumbnail appears, rather than to the right of your layer thumbnail, as when you create a standard layer mask or adjustment layer), and then press Command-I (PC: Ctrl-I) to Invert the layer mask and hide the brighter shadows adjustment behind a black layer mask.

Step 20:

Now it's the same ol' routine of painting over the camera (with the Brush tool, in white) to reveal the brighter version of the dark camera (as shown here). Compare how the camera looks here with the camera in the previous step, and you can see what a dramatic improvement this made. Look at the detail in the camera that was lost in the shadows in the previous versions.

Step 21:

Go ahead and flatten the layers again, and now let's add some finishing touches, starting with burning in the edges. Once you've flattened, duplicate the Background layer, and change the layer blend mode to Multiply to make the layer much darker. Then press M to get the Rectangular Marquee tool, and make a selection that is inset about 1" from the edges of the document (as seen here). To greatly soften our selection, go under the Select menu, under Modify, and choose Feather. When the Feather Selection dialog appears, enter 250 pixels (for a high-res image, as we have here) and click OK to add the maximum amount of edge softening.

Step 22:

Now press Delete (PC: Backspace) to knock a soft-edged hole out of the top, darker layer, which reveals the center of the non-darkened layer below (the edges of the bottom layer are hidden by the top layer—that's how we get the burned-in edge effect). Go ahead and press Command-D (PC: Ctrl-D) to Deselect and toggle this layer on/off a couple of times (by clicking on the Eye icon to the left of the Background copy layer's thumbnail), so you can see what a dramatic difference this burned-in edge effect makes.

Step 23:
Now you can flatten the layers, step back and look at the photo, and ask yourself that question we asked in Step 17, again. At this point, I like everything but one thing: to me, the whole photo looks a little too yellow—especially in the flesh tones. Luckily, that's an easy fix. Press Command-U (PC: Ctrl-U) to bring up the Hue/Saturation dialog. At the top of the dialog, from the Edit pop-up menu, choose Yellows (so we can adjust just the yellow in the photo). Drag the Saturation slider to the left, looking at your photo as you drag, and keep dragging until the flesh tones look better (I had to go all the way down to –36 to make it look right on my monitor). Then click OK.

Step 24:
Now you can apply your sharpening, so go to the Actions panel and apply some high sharpening (as shown here).

Step 25:

Now that we've applied our sharpening, we're going to use a trick to make that camera look super-sharp. We're going to use another layer mask in the same way we've been doing to "paint with light," but this time we're going to "paint with sharpening." Start by duplicating the Background layer, then go to the Filter menu and choose Unsharp Mask from the top of the Filter menu (or just press Command-F [PC: Ctrl-F]. The last filter you used automatically appears at the top of the Filter menu for your convenience, as shown here). This applies a second pass of that sharpening, and now the photo probably looks too sharp in most places.

Step 26:

Option-click (PC: Alt-click) on the Add Layer Mask icon at the bottom of the Layers panel to add a black layer mask to this oversharpened layer.

Step 27:

Get the Brush tool, and with your Foreground color set to white, paint over just the camera to reveal the extra sharpening on it, which makes it really look crisp, but keeps the rest of the photo with only that one initial pass of sharpening. Continue to paint with sharpening over the barrel and the camera body until the camera is super-sharp (like the one shown here). Then flatten the layers and you're done. The final before and after images are shown below.

Before

After

LESSON 15

I was shooting out at Point Lobos, near Carmel, California, and about 15 minutes before sunset, the sun ducked behind a huge wall of clouds, never to be seen again, so the shoot was pretty much over. However, as I was walking back to my rental car, I saw the one decent shot I would get that day—one of my rental car (sad, I know). Anyway, although the light on everything else was very unremarkable, the light on the car rocked, and with a little 7-Point tweaking, and some creative layer masking and blending, we can make this puppy sing.

Step One:

Open the unadjusted original RAW photo in Camera Raw.

SCOTT KELBY

Step Two:

Let's start by enhancing the "shot at sunset" effect by dragging the Temperature slider over to the right, towards yellow (I dragged it over to 8100).

Step Three:
Now, let's bring out some highlights and brighten the overall image by dragging the Exposure slider a little to the right, over to +0.65. (Remember to keep an eye on the histogram when you make an adjustment like this, and be careful not to let your graph hit the right wall of the histogram, where you start losing high-light detail.)

Step Four:
To bring back our color saturation, and enhance the shadow areas, drag the Blacks slider to the right (as shown here, where I increased the Blacks amount to 22). Since the car itself is black, be careful not to darken it so much that the car starts to lose a lot of detail.

Step Five:
This is the perfect type of image to add clarity to, as it has lots of well-defined edges. Drag the Clarity slider over to the right to around 35.

Step Six:

After we increased the Clarity amount, we picked up a tiny bit of highlight clipping in the Red channel (look back at the histogram in Step Five, and you'll see the highlight clipping warning has turned red). This is an easy fix: just drag the Recovery slider a little to the right until that clipping warning goes away (here, I dragged to 8). Then, to make the colors a little more vibrant, drag the Vibrance slider to the right (to +18).

Step Seven:

Click on the Tone Curve icon in the panel area (the second from the left), and to increase the contrast in the photo, click on the Point tab, then choose Strong Contrast from the Curve pop-up menu (as shown here).

Step Eight:

Since this is the kind of image that can handle a lot of sharpening (it's shiny and metallic with lots of well-defined edges), let's increase the amount of sharpening that's applied to the image at this capture stage. Click on the Detail icon in the panel area and increase the Amount to 70. Then, to exaggerate the amount of sharpening, drag the Detail slider to the right to 50 (the Detail slider controls how much "halo prevention" is turned on. Photoshop's regular Unsharp Mask filter creates little halos around the edges if you sharpen something aggressively. The Detail slider in Camera Raw is set at 25 by default, which prevents halos quite a bit, so by increasing the Detail amount, you're taking your chances at punching up the "oomph" of your sharpening. I wouldn't do this with portraits, but with a photo like this that can handle loads of sharpening, I raise the Detail amount).

Step Nine:

Now we're going to add the burned-in edge vignette, but we're going to add it right here in Camera Raw. Why am I choosing to do it now, here in Camera Raw, rather than later, using layers in Photoshop like in other parts of the book? It's only because I can see, right now, while I'm still in Camera Raw, that I want to darken the edges and get that soft-spotlight effect. There's no big advantage, except it's just easier to do it here. Click on the Lens Corrections icon, then under Lens Vignetting, drag the Amount slider (which controls how dark the edges get) quite a ways over to the left to –68. Then, drag the Midpoint slider (which controls how far into the photo your burned edges extend) almost all the way over to the left to 7. That's it (I told you it was easier).

Step 10:

Now click the Open Image button to open the photo in Photoshop. The first thing I would do is darken up the windows, so you can't see inside as much and it doesn't distract your eye from the subject, which is the outside of the car. Get the Quick Selection tool (W) and start painting over the windshield, and it will quickly select the area for you. If it selects a little too much, it's not a big deal because you're just going to be doing a little bit of darkening here—nothing too drastic.

Step 11:

Click (or paint a stroke) over the side windows to select them, too. It will probably also select the divider between the front and back windows, but as I said, in this instance, it's not a big deal. If it does select much more than you'd like, just press-and-hold the Option (PC: Alt) key and paint over the area you want to remove from your selection.

Step 12:

Once you have the windows selected, press Command-L (PC: Ctrl-L) to bring up the Levels dialog. When the dialog appears, drag the bottom-right (white Output Levels) slider to the left (as shown here, where I dragged it down to 184) to darken your selected areas. (*Note:* The reason we used this slider, rather than darkening the shadows or midtones using the top Input Levels sliders, is because either one of those would also saturate the colors a bit. This lower-right slider darkens without saturating the color.) When it looks dark enough to you, click OK and press Command-D (PC: Ctrl-D) to Deselect.

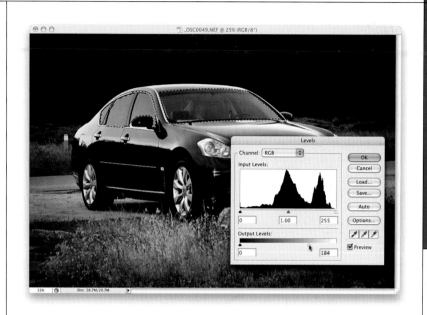

Step 13:

Now it's time to make that chrome really shine (I use this trick anytime I want the brighter parts of a photo to be brighter—this isn't just a "chrome only" trick). Start by duplicating the Background layer by dragging it onto the Create a New Layer icon, then change the blend mode of this layer to Screen to make it very bright.

Step 14:

We're only going to reveal the chrome areas of the car, so you'll need to hide this brighter Screen layer behind a black layer mask. To do that, press-and-hold the Option (PC: Alt) key and click on the Add Layer Mask icon at the bottom of the Layers panel.

Step 15:

Make sure your Foreground color is set to white, get the Brush tool (B), choose a soft-edged brush from the Brush Picker, and start painting over the wheels, the headlights, the chrome on the grill—anything you want to be brighter and to really stand out.

Step 16:

Paint over all the areas you want brighter, then lower the Opacity setting of this brighter layer until the brightness of these areas looks good to you and is realistic with the rest of the image (in this case, I had to lower it down to 50%, until it looked nicely blended in with the rest of the car. After all, you don't want it to look like you enhanced those areas—you just want them to be enhanced. So be careful not to overdo this type of retouching by leaving all your edits at 100% strength).

Step 17:

Now step back, look at the photo, and ask yourself, "What do I wish were different in this image?" Personally, I don't like the fact that the wheels look so yellow. This may have been exactly what they looked like at the time, but I just don't like it. I'd rather see much less of that yellow color in the wheels. To do that, start by getting the Elliptical Marquee tool (press Shift-M until you have it), then click-and-drag out an oval-shaped selection around the front wheel (as shown here). There's a trick you can use to help you get your oval positioned directly over the wheel, and that is once you start dragging out your oval—as soon as you see that it's not exactly over the wheel, before you let go of the mouse button—just use your thumb to hold down the Spacebar on the keyboard. That lets you reposition the oval as you're dragging it and resizing it. It's much easier now.

Step 18:

Once the first wheel is selected, press-and-hold the Shift key and select the back wheel, as well (holding the Shift key lets you add another selection to your current selection). Don't forget the ol' Spacebar trick when trying to select that back wheel. Once both wheels are selected, click on the top layer's image thumbnail (instead of the layer mask) and press Command-U (PC: Ctrl-U) to bring up the Hue/Saturation dialog. Choose Yellows from the Edit pop-up menu at the top, then drag the Saturation slider to the left to around –51 to greatly reduce the yellow tint in the wheels (as seen here). Click OK, and you can then deselect by pressing Command-D (PC: Ctrl-D).

Step 19:

Now let's do some retouching to remove distracting elements from the scene. First, flatten your layers by choosing Flatten Image from the Layers panel's flyout menu, then let's get rid of that distracting post to the left of the back of the car (see Step 18 for a reminder of what that post looks like). Get the Clone Stamp tool (S), press-and-hold the Option (PC: Alt) key and click once just to the left of the post to sample the grass and shrubs in that area. Then move your cursor over the post itself and begin painting. This clones the area you sampled right over the post.

Step 20:

Let's extend (clone over) the grassy area in the bottom-left corner of the image, covering over those distracting gaps. Take the Clone Stamp tool, press-and-hold the Option (PC: Alt) key, and sample in the grass to the right of that open area, then begin painting over the gaps and rocks on the left side (as shown here). In just a minute or two, you'll have it covered over. (*Note:* You may have to resample a few times to cover the area without making the fix obvious.)

Step 21:

The last thing I would remove is the license plate up front. It kind of spoils the whole look of the car. Using the Clone Stamp tool again, sample to the right of the license plate, right on the black part of the bumper, then begin cloning the black bumper over the bottom of the license plate. Why only the bottom? Because the top is a little trickier.

Step 26:

Set your Foreground color to white, get the Brush tool (B), choose a soft-edged brush from the Brush Picker, and start painting over background areas you want to be out-of-focus (as shown here).

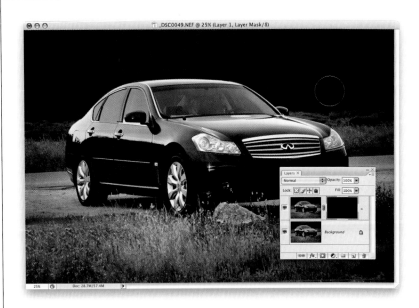

Step 27:

When it's time to paint the grass right up by the road, it wouldn't be as blurry as the tree far behind it. So, go up to the Options Bar and lower the Opacity of your Brush tool to around 50% (or less), and then paint over that grass, so those areas will be less blurry.

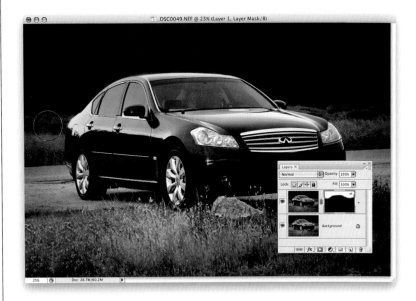

Step 28:

Now it's time to sharpen using your Sharpen High action (the one you created way back in Lesson 1), so go to your Actions panel, click on it, then click the Play Selection icon at the bottom of the panel. The before and after images are shown below.

Before

After

LESSON 16

You're 15 lessons into this now, so I'm going to start backing off on telling you every little thing about every single step, because by now you pretty much have a feel for what's happening. So, over the next few lessons, expect less hand-holding, and more just straight direction on what to do next. This was a lifestyle shot from my book, *The iPhone Book*, and it was shot on (what was supposed to look like) a white seamless background. We use just about the whole System, and then some, to get this image to where it could be included in the book, but that's just what you have to do sometimes.

Step One:
Open the unadjusted original RAW photo in Camera Raw.

SCOTT KELBY

Step Two:
We'll start by fixing the white balance. This was shot on a white background, but the background looks yellowish and dull because the white balance is off. This is an easy one to fix—just get the White Balance tool (I) from the toolbar up top, and click it once anywhere on the background (as shown here) and the white balance problem is fixed.

Step Three:
Now let's brighten the overall image by dragging the Exposure slider over to the right to around +1.05.

Step Four:
Next, let's boost the amount of blacks in the deepest shadow areas by dragging the Blacks slider over to the right to around 8. Then, click the Open Image button to open the photo in Photoshop, and we'll do some retouching and sharpening there.

Step Five:
Let's do just a little retouching on her face. Start by duplicating the Background layer (press Command-J on a Mac or Ctrl-J on a PC). We're going to remove a tiny blemish just above the corner of her smile, so you may want to get the Zoom tool (Z) and zoom in on that area. Then, get the Healing Brush tool from the Toolbox (or press Shift-J until you have it), press-and-hold the Option (PC: Alt) key, and click once just to the right of the tiny blemish (as shown here) to sample that area.

Step Six:

Now move your cursor over the blemish and just click once, and the blemish is gone. Move around the rest of her face and remove any other tiny blemishes (it should just take you a minute or two at best).

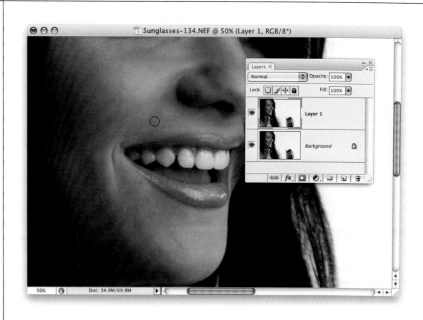

Step Seven:

Once any blemishes are removed (we always do this first), let's do an overall skin smoothing technique. Start by going to the Layers panel's flyout menu and choosing Flatten Image, then duplicate the Background layer again. Go under the Filter menu, under Blur, and choose Gaussian Blur. When the Gaussian Blur filter dialog appears, increase the Radius to 20 pixels (so the photo is very blurry) and click OK.

Step Eight:

Now, lower the Opacity setting of this blurry layer to 40%. This definitely smoothes her skin, but it smoothes everything else, too, and we only want her skin smoothed. In the next step, we'll "paint with blur" to put the softness just on her skin, and not on her hair, or the iPhone, or her shirt, etc.

Step Nine:

Press-and-hold the Option (PC: Alt) key and click on the Add Layer Mask icon at the bottom of the Layers panel to hide the soft, blurry layer behind a black layer mask. Now set your Foreground color to white, get the Brush tool (B), choose a soft-edged brush, and start painting over her skin (as shown here). Avoid any areas that are supposed to have detail, like her eyelashes, eyebrows, lips, teeth, hair, nostrils, or any edge areas that are supposed to be sharp. Use the Left Bracket key ([) and Right Bracket key (]) to quickly make your brush smaller or larger, respectively.

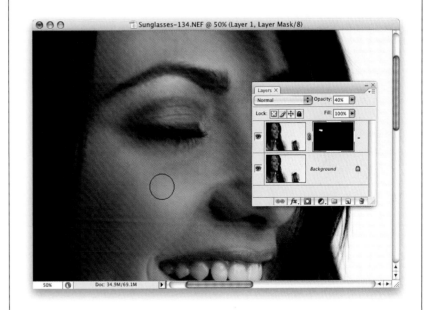

Step 10:

Continue painting until all her skin areas are smoothed. At this point, if you think her skin should be even softer, you could raise the Opacity setting of the blurry layer up to 50% (for this image, I don't think it needs to be that high. In fact, we could probably get away with as little as 30%, or even 20% opacity, but here I left it at 40%). Once it looks good to you, flatten the layers.

Step 11:

Now that the layers are flattened, what's next? Let's open up some of the detail in her hair by opening up the shadow areas. Duplicate the Background layer, then go under the Filter menu and choose Convert for Smart Filters. (*Note:* The reason I always have you duplicate the layer, then convert it for Smart Filters is so we can apply the Shadow/Highlight command as if it were an adjustment layer. By doing it this way, we get some of the same functionality as if it were an adjustment layer, including the ability to change our settings after the fact, hide them from view, or remove them altogether, plus we get a layer mask with it, as well.)

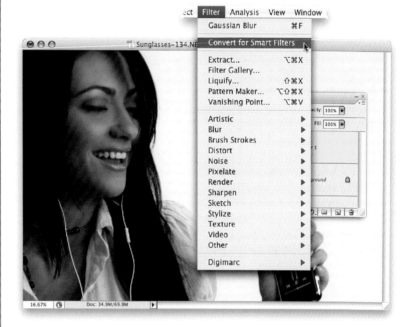

Step 12:
Go under the Image menu, under Adjustments, and choose Shadow/Highlight. When you open the Shadows/Highlights dialog, the default setting opens up the shadows by 50%, which is just about always way too much, and here it is (you guessed it) way too much. So, drag the Shadows Amount slider down to around 18%, until her hair has more detail and highlights (like you see here), then click OK.

Step 13:
Another adjustment-layer-like feature is the fact that after you apply the Shadow/Highlight adjustment, you can control the amount by lowering the layer opacity (here I lowered it to 68%, so it doesn't look too obvious and blends into the rest of the photo naturally). Once you're satisfied, flatten your image. Now, step back and look at the photo. What do you wish were different? I'm hoping you're thinking that the iPhone, which is an important part of this photo, looks kind of washed out (well, at least the image in the iPhone looks washed out).

Step 14:

We're going to darken the image in the iPhone by choosing Curves from the Create New Adjustment Layer pop-up menu at the bottom of the Layers panel. When the dialog appears, choose Strong Contrast (RGB) from the Preset pop-up menu. Click OK to apply this steep curve, which creates a lot of contrast in the whole image (of course, we only need that much contrast in the iPhone's screen, but that's why we chose Curves as an adjustment layer, rather than just applying it directly from the Image menu, under Adjustments).

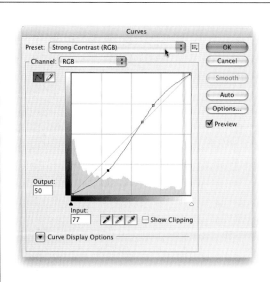

Step 15:

Now press Command-I (PC: Ctrl-I) to Invert the layer mask and hide the strong contrast curve effect behind a black mask. Make sure your Foreground color is set to white, get the Brush tool, and paint over the iPhone's screen (not the black sections at the top and bottom—just paint over the color screen. The reason you don't want to paint over the top and bottom is it'll turn those to solid black, and you want to keep some detail in those areas).

Step 16:

We do want to add some contrast to those black top and bottom areas of the iPhone, but we don't want that much contrast. So, simply go up to the Options Bar and lower the Opacity setting of the Brush tool to around 70% (or lower). Now you can paint over those areas (as shown here), and not have them turn solid black and lose all their detail.

Step 17:

Now ask yourself, "Is that iPhone screen looking good? Does it need to have a little more contrast to make that screen really pop?" (Answer to yourself, "Yes," or this project is going to end right here.) You can do this incredibly easily because you applied Curves as an adjustment layer. Just go back to the Layers panel, double-click on the Curves adjustment layer thumbnail, and the dialog opens with the settings you had applied. To add more contrast in the shadow areas, click on the bottom-most point on the curve and just drag it straight downward and watch how it affects your iPhone screen as you drag down. When the screen looks nice and saturated, click OK.

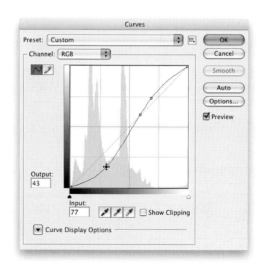

Step 18:

Go ahead and flatten your layers, then let's apply some medium sharpening to the entire image using the Sharpen Medium action you created earlier.

Step 19:

Now let's make that iPhone and it's screen really "pop" by spot-sharpening just that area. Duplicate the Background layer, then apply the medium Unsharp Mask filter to this layer two more times, using the same settings (you can choose it from the top of the Filter menu, as shown here, or press Command-F [PC: Ctrl-F] twice). Then, hide that oversharp-ened layer behind a black layer mask by pressing-and-holding the Option (PC: Alt) key and clicking on the Add Layer Mask icon at the bottom of the Layers panel.

Step 20:

Get the Brush tool (your Foreground color should still be white), and paint over just the iPhone itself. You'll get away with oversharpening this iPhone because it's metallic, shiny, and has lots of well-defined edges. Once you've painted over the iPhone (and the headphone plug), go ahead and flatten the image, since we're done. The before and after images follow.

Before

After

LESSON 17

This one's fun because after we apply as much of the 7-Point System as we need, we get to apply a nice "Hollywood Look" effect in Photoshop that takes the image to a whole 'nother level. The cowboy here is actually sitting on a horse (which has nothing to do with our image editing—I just thought you'd want to know), and he's backlit against a gray sky, so there are plenty of challenges here to keep you busy. I was able to throw a little light back into his face by using a reflector, but it just wasn't enough to do the job. I guess that's why Adobe invented Photoshop.

Step One:
Open the unadjusted original RAW photo in Camera Raw. Let's make the photo a little less yellow by dragging the Temperature slider to the left (towards blue). Here, I lowered the white balance temperature to 5100.

Step Two:
Now, if you look at the histogram in the previous step, you'll see the highlight clipping warning is turned on (in the top right of the histogram)—it's white, which lets us know that we have some highlight clipping (loss of detail in the extreme highlights). So, to bring those highlights back, we're going to drag the Recovery slider to the right until the highlight warning turns solid black (here, I dragged to 19).

SCOTT KELBY

Step Three:

To add a little fill light to his face, drag the Fill Light slider just a little to the right (I dragged it to 13) to open up the shadow areas. (*Note:* He's backlit with the sun behind him, so his face would have been very dark, but I had an assistant holding a 30" reflector to bounce some light back onto his face.)

Step Four:

Now let's boost the deepest shadow areas by dragging the Blacks slider over to the right to around 13.

Step Five:

Let's add some snap and punch (which would make a great name for a breakfast cereal) to our image by dragging the Clarity slider to the right to 40. To really see the Clarity slider's effect, zoom in to a 100% view (as we have here).

Step Six:

Now, return to a fit-in-window view (by choosing Fit in View from the magnification pop-up menu in the bottom-left corner of the window), and let's add some serious contrast by going to the Tone Curve panel (click on the second icon from the left in the panel area). When it appears, click on the Point tab, and then choose Strong Contrast from the Curve pop-up menu.

Step Seven:

Lastly, click on the Detail icon (the third icon from the left in the panel area), and let's increase the Amount of sharpening to 58. If this were a portrait of a woman, I would have increased the Masking amount, so just the edge areas would get the sharpening, and not her skin. But in this case, with a rugged cowboy, you want to accentuate the texture of his skin, so we leave the Masking set at 0. Now click Open Image to open the photo in Photoshop.

Step Eight:

After all that, his face is still kind of dark. The reason I didn't go back and just increase the Fill Light amount back in Camera Raw is that it puts fill light into all the shadow areas—not just in his face. So there's no way to control where the fill light is applied—it's applied to the entire photo. However, in Photoshop, using a Smart Filters layer with a Shadow/Highlight adjustment, we can paint with light and control exactly where the fill light falls. So, press Command-J (PC: Ctrl-J) to duplicate the Background layer, then go under the Filter menu and choose Convert for Smart Filters.

Step Nine:

Go under the Image menu, under Adjustments, and choose Shadow/Highlight. When the dialog appears, lower the Shadows Amount to around 20% (as shown here). Of course, this adds fill light to the entire photo (including his coat, his hat, etc.), but we'll fix that in the next step. For now, just click OK.

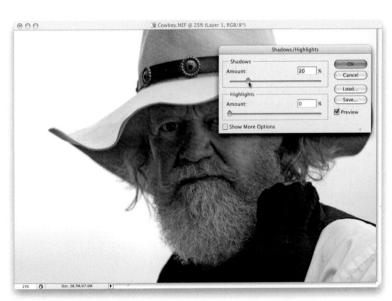

Step 10:

One downside of using Shadow/Highlight is that while it opens up the shadows, in many cases it also intensifies the color in those shadow areas, which generally doesn't look that good. So, if you notice that, after opening up the shadow areas, the color in those shadow areas now looks bad, or is too saturated (which is fairly likely), then go to the Layers panel and change the top layer's blend mode to Luminosity (as shown here). This applies the Shadow/Highlight control to just the detail channel, and not the color channels, which lets you sidestep the problem just like we do when we apply the Unsharp Mask filter.

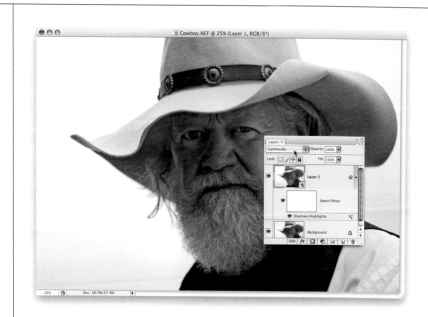

Step 11:

So, you just learned an advantage of applying Shadow/Highlight to a Smart Filters layer, and that is the ability to change the blend mode to Luminosity to avoid color problems. Another advantage (and the main reason we chose to apply Shadow/Highlight to a Smart Filters layer) is that we can use the layer mask of the Smart Filters layer to apply our fill light (shadows) adjustment where we want it. To do that, first click on the Smart Filters layer mask thumbnail, and press Command-I (PC: Ctrl-I) to Invert your mask and hide your shadows adjustment behind a black mask. Then, with your Foreground color set to white, press B to get the Brush tool, choose a large, soft-edged brush, and just paint over his face to reveal the shadows adjustment.

Step 12:

Another advantage is that you can now dial-in just the right amount of shadow fill light by lowering the opacity of this Smart Filters layer. Go ahead and lower the Opacity amount to around 51% to balance out this fill light with the rest of the photo (the last thing you want to do is make it obvious that you lightened this area). Now go ahead and flatten your layers.

Step 13:

Next, we're going to apply a "Hollywood Look" effect that is incredibly popular in Hollywood movie posters. You start by duplicating the Background layer, then remove the color from this duplicate layer by pressing Command-Shift-U (PC: Ctrl-Shift-U), which is the shortcut for the Desaturate command.

Step 18:

Now change the Curves adjustment layer's blend mode to Luminosity. Then, press Command-I (PC: Ctrl-I) to Invert the layer mask and hide your brighter midtones adjustment behind a black layer mask. Switch your Foreground color to white, get the Brush tool again, and paint over his face (as shown here) to reveal the brighter version. Once again, after you've painted in his face, you can control how intense the brightening is by lowering the opacity of this layer (I didn't do it in this case, but it's just nice to know that you could).

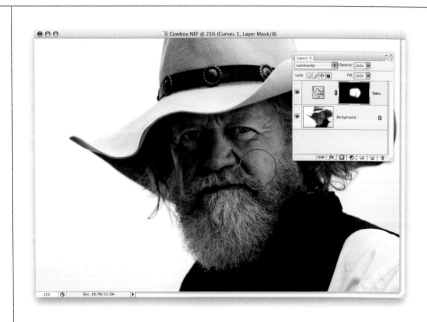

Step 19:

Go ahead and flatten your layers again, then let's apply some noise (the final step to the Hollywood effect). Go under the Filter menu, under Noise, and choose Add Noise. When the Add Noise filter dialog appears, for Amount choose 6% (for a high-resolution image like this), then for Distribution choose Gaussian. The kind of noise you want is grayscale noise (not those red, green, and blue dots produced by digital cameras shooting at high ISOs), so make sure you turn on the Monochromatic checkbox at the bottom of the dialog, then click OK. (*Note:* Be careful not to add too much noise—just enough so it's visible—because when you add sharpening in the next step, it amplifies any noise you've added to the image.)

Step 20:

Lastly, let's apply some heavy sharpening to the image to finish it off, using the Sharpen High action you created back in Lesson 1. The before and after images are shown below.

Before

After

LESSON 18

As I mentioned earlier, I'm really going to back off with the detailed instructions now, because you know what to do. Now I'm just leading the way, like I would with an assistant in my studio. This image was taken on a tender coming back from a shoot on Coco Cay in the Bahamas. The boat was rocking, so the shot isn't exactly tack sharp, but what will make it good is making the sky really dark and dramatic. When I took the shot late in the day, you could see some rain clouds moving in, but a lot of that got lost in the exposure, so we'll use The System to bring it back and then some.

Step One:
Open an unadjusted original RAW photo in Camera Raw (as shown here).

SCOTT KELBY

Step Two:
It's hard to tell if the white balance needs to be changed or not at this point, so let's just start with darkening the sky, and we'll see if we even need to deal with white balance at all. To make the sky darker and more dramatic, start by lowering the Exposure quite a bit (I lowered it to –1.40 here).

Step Three:
There are still some hot spots in that sky, so crunch it down by increasing the Recovery amount big time (I increased it to 53).

Step Four:
Now kick up the Blacks amount to 27, so the sea and sky get real rich in the shadows.

Step Five:
Let's add some snap and punch by dragging the Clarity slider to the right quite a bit (I dragged it to 54 here).

Step Six:

To make the colors pop a bit more, drag the Vibrance slider to the right (to +28).

Step Seven:

Click on the Tone Curve icon (the second icon from the left) at the top of the panel area, then click on the Point tab, and choose the Strong Contrast preset from the Curve pop-up menu to add quite a bit of contrast to the photo (take a look at how those dark clouds are starting to form. Looks like a storm is coming. Let's move the storm closer in the next step).

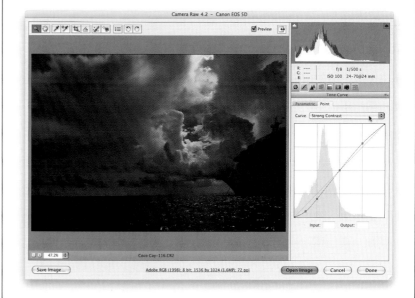

Step Eight:

Click on the top-right point, and move it up a few notches using the Up Arrow key on your keyboard to make your highlights brighter, the curve steeper, and the photo have more contrast. Now, do the same thing to the shadows by clicking on the second-from-the-bottom point, and moving it down a few notches with the Down Arrow key. Now you have darker shadows, an even steeper curve, and even more contrast. It's "Contrastapalooza." Press-and-hold the Shift key, and click on the Open Object button to open the image in Photoshop as a Smart Object.

Step Nine:

We're doing this (opening it as a Smart Object) so we can double-process the photo, so duplicate the Smart Object layer by Control-clicking (PC: Right-clicking) on the layer and choosing New Smart Object via Copy (as shown here).

Note: Just a reminder: if you're lost, or this doesn't sound really familiar, then you're not quite ready for this lesson where I'm just telling you what to do without the detailed descriptions I included in the previous lessons. There's nothing wrong with not being ready for this yet—you just need to review a little bit more, do a few more of the earlier lessons, and then when you're a little more comfortable, jump back here and you'll be able to get through it without a problem.

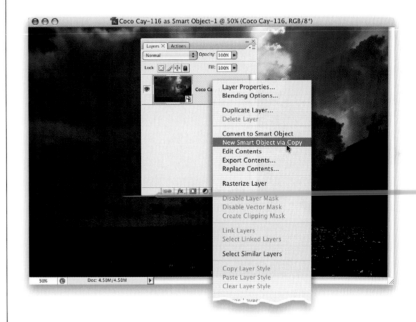

Step 10:

When this duplicate Smart Object layer appears in the Layers panel, double-click directly on its thumbnail to open this layer in Camera Raw. Now we need to brighten the ship and the water, and a quick way to get there is to do something we haven't done even once in the entire book—click the Auto button (as shown here). The reason we haven't done this so far is I think it generally overexposes the photo (it doesn't blow out the highlights, but it pushes the exposure so far that most folks I know think it greatly over-exposes the image). Take a look at the sky—it's not clipping, but it looks like it is. Anyway, we'll just use this auto correction as a starting point.

Step 11:

We don't want to crush down the highlights in the ship or sea, so lower that Recovery amount down to 0, then increase the Fill Light amount so it opens up the shadows in the boat and sea a bit (here, I increased it to 30). Now click OK to apply these changes to our duplicate layer back in Photoshop.

Step 12:

Now hide that brighter Smart Object layer behind a black layer mask. Get the Brush tool, choose a soft-edged brush, set your Foreground color to white, and start painting over the sea to reveal that brighter layer (as I'm doing here).

Step 13:

Keep painting until the brighter sea is painted in, and then carefully paint over the ship, as well. I had to zoom in pretty close, and use a small brush, to paint in the top and front of the ship.

Step 14:

If this ship looks too bright (it does), then lower the layer's Opacity to around 80%, so it blends in.

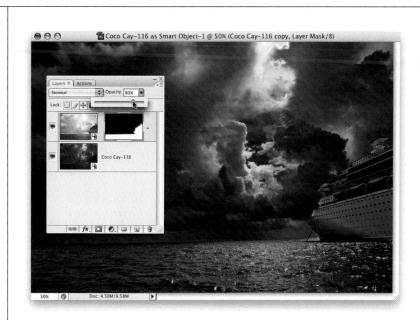

Step 15:

Now, add a Curves adjustment layer, and choose Medium Contrast (RGB) from the Preset pop-up menu in the Curves dialog to add a little more pop to the contrast (I'm really going for that contrasty look, eh?). Click OK to close the dialog.

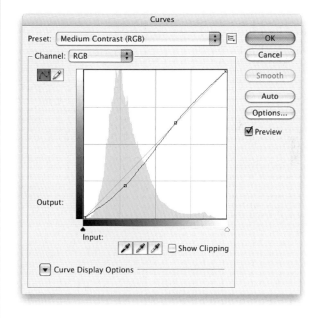

Step 16:

That Curves adjustment did a nice job on the sky and sea, but it made the ship a bit too dark, so take advantage of the Curves adjustment layer's mask by using the Brush tool to paint in black over the ship and hide that Curves contrast adjustment you added in the last step (as shown here).

Step 17:

Now let's create a new layer that's a flattened version of the document, and we'll apply a Shadow/Highlight adjustment to it to lighten up the sky a bit. Press Command-Option-Shift-E (PC: Ctrl-Alt-Shift-E) to create that flattened layer up at the top of the layer stack.

Step 18:

Then, go under the Filter menu and choose Convert for Smart Filters. Bring up the Shadows/Highlights dialog. We're going to dig into the advanced options, so turn on the Show More Options check-box, as seen here.

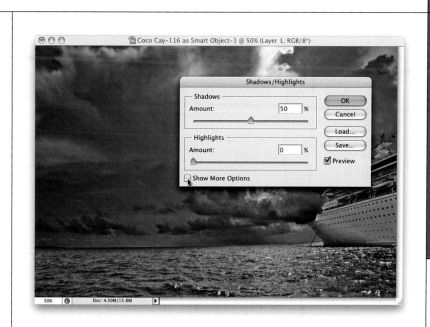

Step 19:

The main reason I use these expanded options is because sometimes (okay, pretty often), when you open up the shadows, it looks kind of, well…fakey. It looks "milky" for lack of a better term, and by going to these advanced options and lowering the Amount (to 25% here), raising the Tonal Width to around 50%, and raising the Radius amount to between 250 and 300 pixels, it looks much more realistic. I don't do this every time—just in situations where opening the shadows does give you that milky look. Go ahead and click OK at this point. Don't forget, we can also change the blend mode for this Smart Filters layer to Luminosity to avoid increasing the colors in the shadow areas.

Step 20:
Click on the Smart Filters layer mask thumbnail, and press Command-I (PC: Ctrl-I) to Invert the mask and hide that opened shadows layer behind a black mask. Now, with the Brush tool active, choose a huge brush, and paint in white over the clouds up higher in the sky to open them up a bit (as shown here). Don't paint near the horizon line—just up high in the sky.

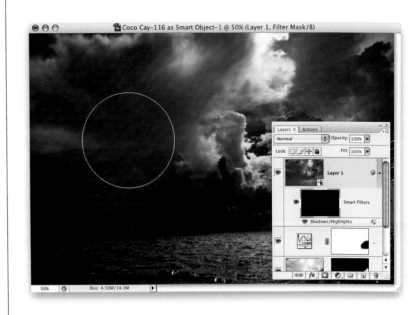

Step 21:
Go ahead and flatten the image and then apply a medium amount of sharpening (using your medium sharpening action). We're going to print this image out, so go ahead and duplicate the Background layer and apply a second pass of sharpening (this is called output, or print, sharpening). If the image looks a little too sharp onscreen, it's probably right on the money, because you lose some of that sharpening that you see onscreen when the image is transferred to photo paper. Then, flatten the image again.

Step 22:

We're going to wrap things up by creating a poster layout for our image. Press Command-N (PC: Ctrl-N) to create a new document, make it 16 inches wide by 20 inches tall, at 240 ppi resolution, and click OK.

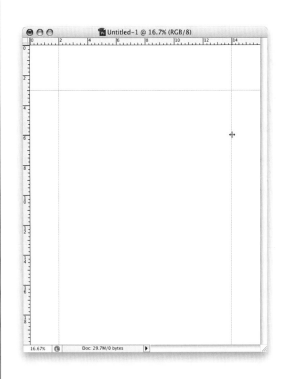

Step 23:

Make your rulers visible by pressing Command-R (PC: Ctrl-R), click inside the left-side ruler and drag out two guides, and position them so there's a 2" margin on either side of the document (as shown here). Then drag out a guide from the top ruler and place it 3" down from the top of the document.

Step 24:

Now get the Move tool (V) and drag-and-drop your ship photo onto this document. Use Free Transform (Command-T [PC: Ctrl-T]) to scale it down so it fits within those margins (as shown here), and then lock in your resizing by pressing the Return (PC: Enter) key. To keep your image proportional, press-and-hold the Shift key while you resize it.

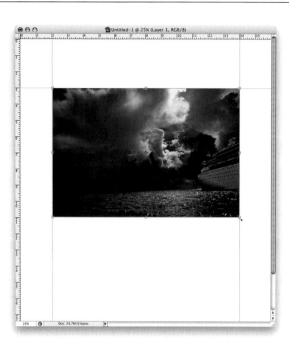

Step 25:

Now we can use the Horizonal Type tool (T) to add some type to finish off the poster look. The type here is in the font Trajan Pro, which gets installed automatically when you install Photoshop CS3 or the entire Creative Suite 3 (so just look in your font list and you'll probably find it there). I added some extra space between the letters to make it look more elegant (this is done by increasing the Tracking amount in Photoshop's Character panel). I also scanned my signature and added it under the bottom-right corner of the photo, and added the letters A/P (for Artist Print) under the bottom-left corner. The before and after images of just the image itself appear on the next page.

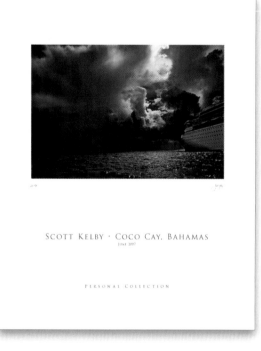

Before

After

LESSON 19

These boats were in a pond up in Maine, and it's really a pretty unremarkable shot (especially with just two boats. One may be the "loneliest number," but in photography, two of anything other than people can make for a graphically boring photo, but we can take care of that, right?). This photo has the whole ball of wax, from too bright of an exposure, to a bad white balance choice, to a pretty lackluster composition.

Step One:
Open the unadjusted original RAW photo in Camera Raw (as shown here).

Step Two:
We want to make this photo look like it was taken closer to dusk, so our first step is to warm up the white balance. Drag the Temperature slider over to 7350 to add more yellow into the image.

Step Three:
Now you'll want to back off the highlight exposure a bit, so it doesn't look like it was taken at high noon. Drag the Exposure slider to the left to –0.60 to darken the exposure a bit.

Step 12:

Get the Move tool (V), and drag the boat copy layer over to fill in that gap (as shown here). Now, let's scale that third boat down just a little bit, both for visual interest and to make it look a little different from the center boat we copied. Press Command-T (PC: Ctrl-T) to bring up Free Transform, press-and-hold the Shift key, grab a corner, and drag inward to scale it down a little in size. Press Return (PC: Enter) to lock in your transformation when you're done.

Step 13:

Now add a layer mask, then with your Foreground color set to black, paint over the excess area around the copied boat (as shown here) to get it to blend in with the rest of the photo. This is easier than it sounds, because most of what you have to do is just erase those brighter areas of water in the very back of the boat. Should take you all of about two minutes, at best.

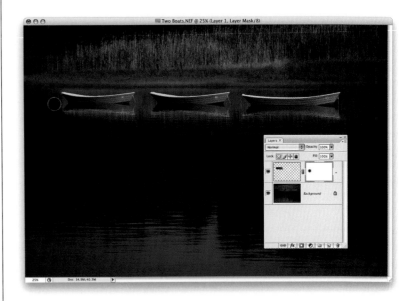

Step 14:
The other area that needs a little blending is just below the boat's reflection— you can see a little line, so make your brush really big (like the one shown here), and gently paint it away. When you're finished, flatten your layers.

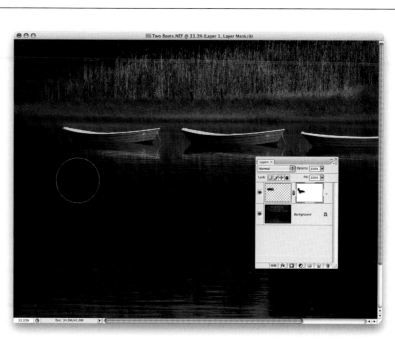

Step 15:
Now you're going to add a rope line to the back of the second boat, so it looks like the three boats are connected (like the front two boats are). First, click on the Background layer, then get the Lasso tool again, and make a selection around the rope line in the back of the first boat (the one on the far right). Then add a 2-pixel feather just to soften the edges of your selection a little bit, and click OK.

Step 16:

Press Command-J (PC: Ctrl-J) to put a copy of that rope up on its own separate layer, then drag that rope over to the back of the center boat and position it on the back of the boat. Just to make it look a little different, you might want to rotate the rope line just a little bit (as seen here, using Free Transform). It's a little thing, but it's all about the little things, right? Press Return (PC: Enter) to lock your rotation in.

Step 17:

Now you're going to have to do some cleanup—similar to what you did with the third boat—and that is to remove the excess water around the rope line you copied from the first boat. This is even easier than before: just add a layer mask, and paint in black around the rope and it blends right in. Piece of cake.

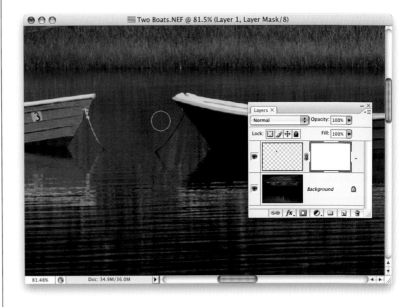

Step 18:

There's one last giveaway that would let someone looking at the photo know that you added a third boat, and that is that the third and second boats both have the exact same number on them (the number 3). So, you'll have to change that (it's easy). First, go ahead and flatten your layers and zoom in on the number on your new boat. Then, get the Polygonal Lasso tool and draw a straight-line selection around the number and its surrounding box on the third boat (the boat you copied). The reason you're putting this selection around the number box is so that you don't accidentally paint or clone outside of it.

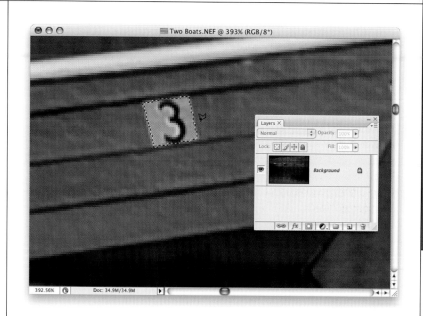

Step 19:

Get the Clone Stamp tool (S), press-and-hold the Option (PC: Alt) key, and click to the left of the number to sample the light-colored background. Now, take the Clone Stamp tool and start painting (cloning) over the number to erase it (clone over it), as shown here.

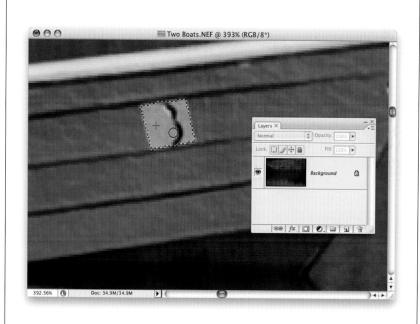

Step 20:

Once you've completely cloned over the number, you can deselect, set your Foreground color to black, get the Horizontal Type tool (T), and type in the number 4 (Arial is a pretty good font for this). Now, you'll need to resize the font, and position the number over the spot where the number 3 used to be. Once it's close to being in place, press Command-Return (PC: Ctrl-Enter) to lock in the layer, then bring up Free Transform and rotate the number a bit (as shown here) so it matches the angle of the original number, then lock in your changes.

Step 21:

Now get the Eyedropper tool (I), scroll over to the first boat, and click the tool right on the number 2 to sample the exact color of that number (that color now becomes your Foreground color). Then scroll back over to your black 4 and press Option-Delete (PC: Alt-Backspace) to fill it with that same exact color. Next, duplicate the number layer. Press D, then X to set your Foreground color to white, then press Option-Delete to fill your duplicate number with white. Drag that layer below your original 4 layer in the Layers panel, then get the Move tool, and hit the Left Arrow key on your keyboard once and the Down Arrow key once to offset the white copy from the original. Lower the Opacity of the white number layer to around 65% (as shown here) so it blends in a little more. That's it—you've fixed the number conti-nuity problem.

Step 22:
Let's warm this photo up even more. Click back on the top Type layer, then choose Photo Filter from the Create New Adjustment Layer pop-up menu, and when the Photo Filter dialog appears, leave it set at the default filter (Warming Filter 85), but increase the Density (amount) to around 60% to make the photo even warmer, then click OK.

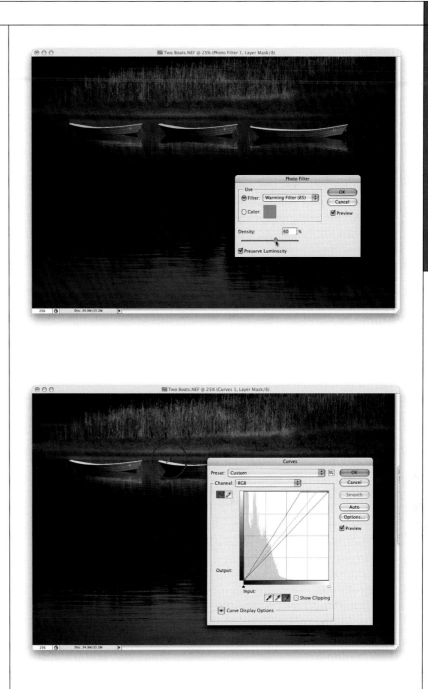

Step 23:
If the boats look too yellow (and I think they're starting to), try this: add a Curves adjustment layer, and when the dialog appears, grab the highlight (far right) Eyedropper and click it once on the top of the center boat (the part that's supposed to be white), and it instantly removes most of the yellowing in our photo. You may like the way the photo looks right now (now that the color cast is gone), and in that case, just click OK, flatten the layers, add some sharpening, and you're done. However, if you like the dusky, warm look, but want the boats not as yellowish, then click OK anyway (but we'll add another step next).

Step 24:

We'll make use of that adjustment layer's mask now. Start by pressing Command-I (PC: Ctrl-I) to Invert the mask, hiding your color-corrected version (see in the previous step) behind a black mask. Now, get the Brush tool, and paint in white over just the boats and their reflections in the water (don't forget the reflections or they will be a dead giveaway that this photo has been retouched).

Step 25:

Keep painting over the boats, and their reflections, until you've painted over all three boats completely (as shown here). Notice how only the boats are gray now, and nothing else—the rest has been left unchanged.

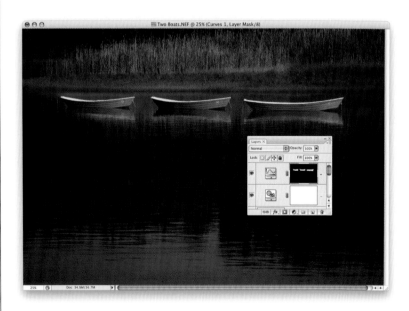

Step 26:
If you want to bleed a little of the surrounding yellow into your boats (and I think you should), then just lower the Opacity setting of this layer to around 68%. This way, the boats aren't so gray that they don't look like they're in this scene, but they're not so yellow that it's distracting. Now you can flatten the image because it's sharpening time.

Step 27:
Go ahead and apply your Sharpen Medium action to the entire image.

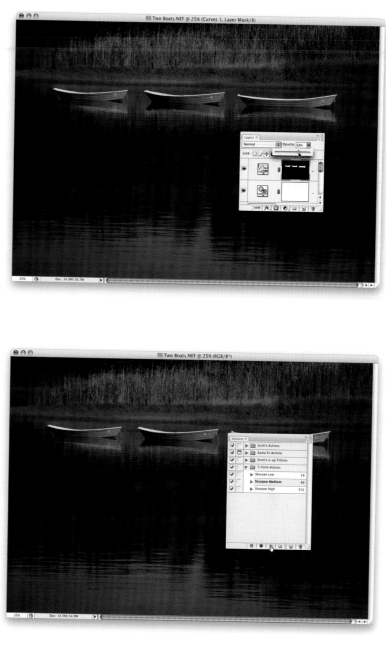

Step 28:

Now, technically—we're done, but I'm going to give you an option that you might want to consider: pano cropping. That's right—crop this photo so it looks like a panorama (or at least has the long, wide cropping ratio of a panorama). You do this by getting the Crop tool (C), then clicking-and-dragging out a long, rectangular crop border (like the one shown here). Then, once it's in position, press Return (PC: Enter) to lock in your cropping. In the next step, we'll add a poster layout to further accentuate the pano look.

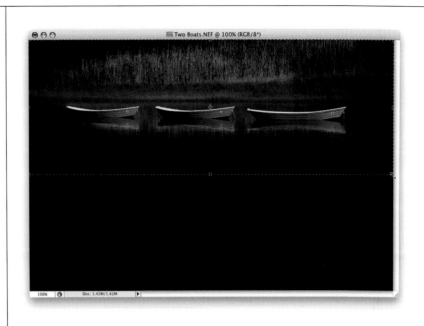

Step 29:

Go under the Image menu and choose Canvas Size. Turn on the Relative checkbox, add 2" of width, 2" of height, choose White as your Canvas Extension Color (from the pop-up menu at the bottom), and click OK. Then go back to that same dialog, this time add 3" of height, but in the Anchor grid, click on the top-center square, so the 3" of white space are added below your current image, which gives you the gallery canvas you see here. Now, lastly, you can add some type. I used the font Trajan Pro, with lots of tracking (space) between the letters, for the top line of type. For the smaller bottom line of type, I used the font Minion Pro Italic (both of these fonts come with Photoshop CS2/CS3) in all lowercase, with lots of spacing between the letters, as well. So, that's the final layout, but a comparison of the original, bright-light, two-boat photo with a more dusky, three-boat photo is on the next page.

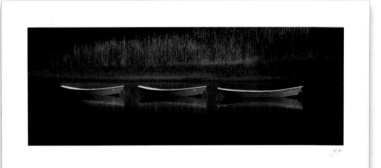

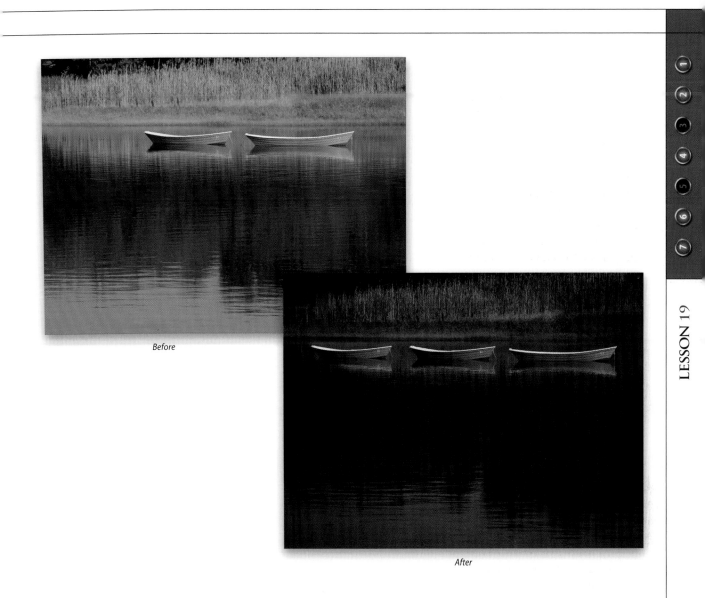

Before

After

LESSON 20

This is one of my favorite shots in the book, partially because I love the water's reflection of the sky, partially because I love how the Lab color move just makes this photo "sing," and partially because I survived the three-mile hike over mountains in 112° desert heat, while lugging a backpack full of camera gear (something I could never have done if I hadn't lost over 100 lbs in the past year). It was a real milestone for me, as I hope this chapter is a milestone for you, because when I mentioned "the Lab color move," you knew what I was talking about. Cool, ain't it?

Step One:
Open the unadjusted RAW photo in Camera Raw (as shown here).

SCOTT KELBY

Step Two:

We can't go too crazy with the white balance here, and we don't want to since the photo was taken outdoors in bright sunlight. So, even if the camera's white balance was set to Auto, it wouldn't be off by much (if any). If you wanted to add a little more warmth, you could drag the Temperature slider to the right, over to around 5900, but I wouldn't go farther than that (especially since we're going to pump up the color and contrast later in Photoshop).

Step Three:

We're clipping a little of the highlights up in those clouds (you can see the white highlight clipping warning triangle in the top right of the histogram in the previous step), so drag the Recovery slider over to the right until the warning goes away. Just to clamp down on those clouds a little, drag the slider a little farther than you really need to (over to around 34) to tone down the whole sky a bit.

Step Four:

Now let's get rid of that washed-out look and bring some rich, saturated color into our shadow areas by dragging the Blacks slider over to around 20. It's already looking much better.

Step Five:

Let's add some midtone snap by zooming in to 100% (double-click on the Zoom tool on the left end of the toolbar), and then dragging the Clarity slider over to the right until it looks nice and punchy (drag it over to around 34).

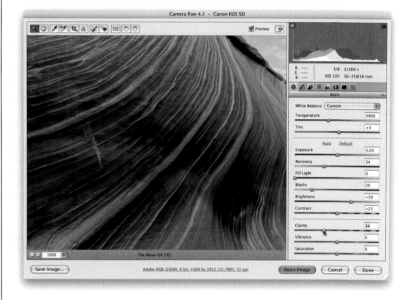

Step Six:

Double-click on the Hand tool (the second tool from the left in the toolbar) to zoom back out so your photo fits into the preview window again. Now drag the Vibrance slider to the right to around +13 to make the colors a bit more vibrant.

Step Seven:

Now head over to the Detail panel, where we'll add some landscape sharpening. Increase the Amount to 70 (these rocks and reflective water can handle a lot of sharpening), and increase the Detail to around 50. Click the Open Image button to open the photo in Photoshop.

Step Eight:

Now let's really make those colors pop by doing a Lab color channels move. Go under the Image menu, under Mode, and choose Lab Color. Then go under the Image menu again and choose Apply Image. When the dialog appears, change the Blending pop-up menu to Soft Light (as shown here), and see how the image looks. Those colors are poppin' all right, but maybe too much. Let's fix that in the next step.

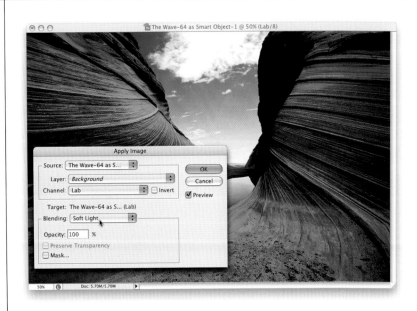

Step Nine:

Lower the Opacity setting to 50%, which basically turns down the amount of the effect by half, and gives you nice, poppin' colors without going too far. Now you can click OK, and then convert back to RGB mode.

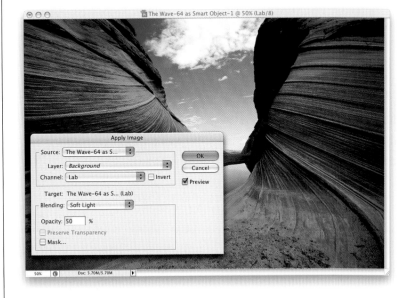

Step 10:

The rocks on the upper-right side of The Wave (as it's called) have gotten pretty dark after all these adjustments, so let's open them up again and bring back that detail. Start by pressing Command-J (PC: Ctrl-J) to duplicate the Background layer, then go under the Filter menu and choose Convert for Smart Filters, so we can apply the Shadow/Highlight control as if it were an adjustment layer.

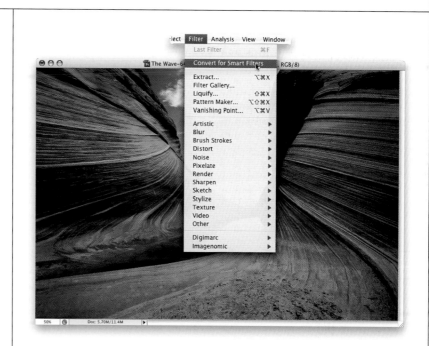

Step 11:

Now go under the Image menu, under Adjustments, and choose Shadow/ Highlight. When the dialog appears, turn on the Show More Options checkbox to see the full set of options. We're just going to adjust the top three (Shadows) sliders: lower the Amount down to 41%, increase the Tonal Width to around 65%, and increase the Radius to 208 pixels, which opens up the shadows in those rocks on the top right without making them look milky and fake. Click OK.

Step 12:

Go to the Layers panel, click on the Smart Filters layer mask thumbnail, and press Command-I (PC: Ctrl-I) to hide your Shadow/Highlight layer behind a black mask (as shown here).

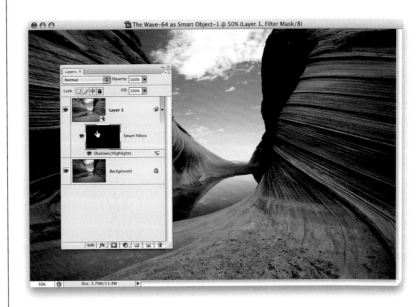

Step 13:

Get the Brush tool, choose a small, soft-edged brush, and with your Foreground color set to white, paint over the rocks on the top right to reveal the opened up shadows version of them (you can see here, those rocks are now out of the shadows and have much more detail than before). But there is a problem, and it's a common problem when applying a Shadow/Highlight adjustment, and that is the rocks themselves are now very red. So, it boosted the shadows, but saturated the color right along with it.

Step 14:

Luckily, fixing that boosted-saturation-in-the-shadows problem couldn't be easier. Just change the blend mode for this layer from Normal to Luminosity, and it bypasses applying the adjustment to the color channels, and only applies it to the luminosity (detail) in the image instead. An easy fix (for a change).

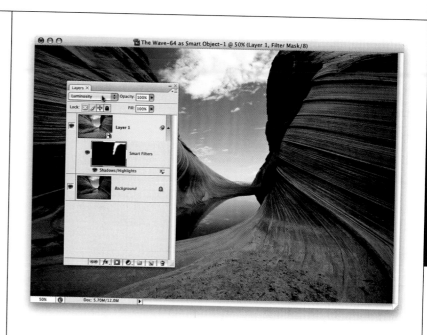

Step 15:

Now the rocks look good. Let's make the sky and the water reflection look as good. Add a Curves adjustment layer. When the Curves dialog appears, click in the center of the curve line to add a point to the center, then drag that point straight down-ward to darken and saturate the midtones in the image.

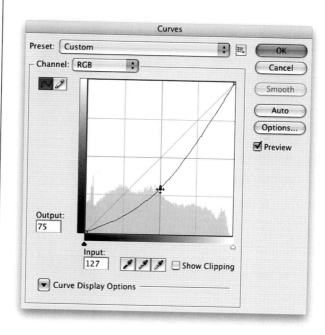

Step 16:

Click OK and the curve is applied, and your entire image has darker midtones. You see where this is going now, don't you? The key phrase was "entire image," and you know (and I know) that we only want the water reflection and the sky to have darker, richer midtones. So....

Step 17:

Press Command-I (PC: Ctrl-I) to Invert the Curves adjustment layer's mask, hiding the darker midtones behind a black mask. Now, get the Brush tool, make sure your Foreground color is set to white, and paint over the water (as shown here) to reveal the darker midtones and really make that water look rich.

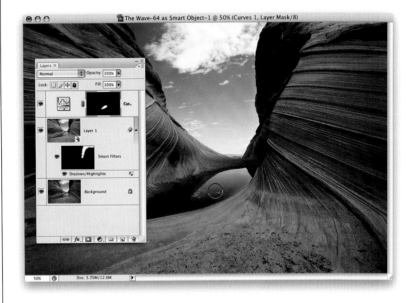

Step 18:

We need to do the same thing to the sky, but rather than painting (and running the risk of accidentally painting over the edges of the rocks), use the Quick Selection tool (W) to paint a few strokes on the sky, and it's quickly selected (as seen here).

Step 19:

Now add a 1-pixel feather, just to help soften and blend the edges a little bit, then click OK.

Step 20:

Press Option-Delete (PC: Alt-Backspace) to fill the selected area of your mask with white, which reveals the darker midtone sky. Of course, once your selection is in place, you could just paint in white to reveal that darker midtone area, because you can't accidentally paint outside the selected area. I just filled the area with white using that keyboard shortcut, simply because it's faster. Press Command-D (PC: Ctrl-D) to Deselect.

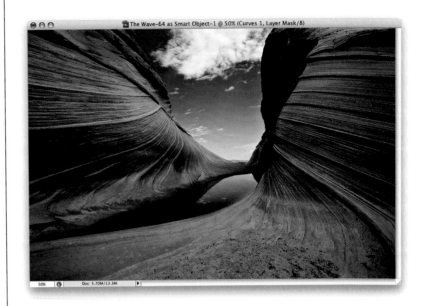

Step 21:

Now, flatten your layers, and then run your Sharpen High action to finish things off. The before and after images are shown on the next page.

Before

After

THE REFRESHER COURSE
LESSON 21

This is the lesson to reach for when you haven't used Photoshop in a while. I'm not talking two or three weeks—I mean two or three months. If you really want to save yourself some frustration, turn back to the beginning and read my "The Seven Points are Revealed Right Here!" section, then come back here. If you do that first, this "Refresher Course" will all make sense, and you'll be back up and running fast (like riding a bike, but one with lots of scary-looking sliders and buttons). There's also a one-page cheat sheet at the end of this lesson.

Step One:

The first point of our 7-Point System is to open the image in Adobe Camera Raw. It doesn't matter if it's a JPEG, TIFF, or was shot in RAW format, we always start by opening the image in Camera Raw because it's the easiest way to adjust the overall tone, color, and contrast of our image. *Note:* If the photo is in RAW format, double-clicking on it will open it in Camera Raw. If it's a JPEG or TIFF image, start by going under Photoshop's File menu and choosing Open (PC: Open As). Then, in the dialog, after you click on the JPEG or TIFF image you want to open, choose Camera Raw from the Format (PC: Open As) pop-up menu, click Open, and the image will open in Camera Raw.

SCOTT KELBY

Step Two:

I always start by adjusting the white balance first (which takes care of most, if not all, of the color problems in the image). If you're adjusting a RAW image, you can start by choosing one of the presets from the White Balance pop-up menu at the top of the Basic panel as a starting point. Then you can tweak the color by dragging the Temperature slider to the left to make the image cooler and more blue, or to the right to make it warmer and more yellow. If your image is a JPEG or TIFF, skip the White Balance menu presets (which are limited for these formats) and just use the Temperature slider (here, I dragged it to the right to 6850).

Step Three:

Next, I (we, you, us) adjust the exposure using the Exposure slider (which because it controls the highlights, has the biggest single effect on the photo). Dragging it to the right (as shown here, where I dragged to +0.65) makes the photo brighter (dragging to the left makes it darker). If you're dragging to the right, keep an eye on the highlight clipping warning triangle in the upper-right corner of the histogram—it should be black. If it turns red (as shown circled here), or white, or any color except black, you're losing detail in your highlights. To see the area that's being clipped, click on the triangle, and those areas will appear in red on your image.

Step Four:

If you see the highlight clipping warning turn any color except for black (as we did in Step Three), you don't have to back off your exposure, instead you can recover those clipped highlights by dragging the Recovery slider to the right (here, I dragged to 19). By the way, always start by setting the Exposure first, and then use the Recovery slider, if necessary. Besides just recovering lost highlights, I also use the Recovery slider to darken lighter skies (it does a surprisingly good job if you drag the slider quite a ways to the right—much more than you'd usually need to bring back clipped highlights).

Step Five:

At this point we've set the white balance and exposure, and recovered the highlights we clipped. Here's the thing: this image was taken just after dawn, but if you look at the image back in Step Four, I made it so bright it was starting to look like afternoon. So let's now darken the exposure by dragging the Exposure slider back to the left until it only reads +0.15 (so it's brighter than it was originally, but not as bright as our first adjustment). Next, let's pull that "darken lighter skies" trick by dragging the Recovery slider to the right to 55.

Step Six:
If the image looks washed out, there's usually a quick fix for that—just pump up the shadow areas by dragging the Blacks slider to the right (here, I dragged to 30), until the color in the image looks saturated and balanced.

Step Seven:
Now, let's add some midtone contrast and sharpening by increasing the Clarity amount. Before adding clarity, you should first double-click on the Zoom tool (the magnifying glass) in the top toolbar to zoom in to a 100% view, so you can see the effect adding clarity will have on your photo. Drag the Clarity slider to the right and keep an eye on your image to see how it looks (you'll rarely have to go above 50; here, I dragged to 28).

Step Eight:

Click on the Detail icon (the third icon from the left) at the top of the panel area to reveal the Detail panel, where we'll add some sharpening. You can leave the other Detail panel settings in place, but increase the Detail amount to around 65 (increasing the Detail amount works well for landscape images like this, which can handle a lot of sharpening). Now that we have the color and exposure balanced, you can click the Open Image button to open the image in Photoshop, where we'll continue our editing.

Step Nine:

Here's the image open in Photoshop. The image looks better than when we started, but it could be a little more contrasty, and an easy way to do that is to use Curves. (*Note:* The color is okay, so we're going to use Curves to create the contrast for us.) Choose Curves from the Layers panel's Create New Adjustment Layer pop-up menu, as shown here (this is the second point of the 7-Point System).

Step 10:

When the Curves dialog appears, we're just going to use one of the built-in Curves presets (that were added in CS3) that increases the contrast. So, choose Medium Contrast (RGB) from the Preset menu at the top of the dialog (as shown here). Click OK, and then go to the Layers panel and choose Flatten Image from the panel's flyout menu.

Note: Technically, since we were going to have to flatten the image anyway (because of what we're doing in the next step), we could have just applied the Curves adjustment directly to the image itself rather than as an adjustment layer. I applied it here as an adjustment layer since we usually apply it as an adjustment layer, so that we get the advantages of having a built-in mask, and the ability to change our mind later. But in this case, it really didn't matter.

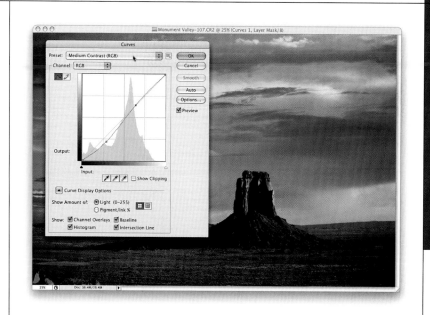

Step 11:

Now we're going to make our colors really pop (and add a bit more contrast) by doing a Lab color channels move (this is the fifth point of the 7-Point System). Go under the Image menu, under Mode, and choose Lab Color (changing to Lab color mode doesn't change the look of the image or damage it in any way). Then, go back under the Image menu and choose Apply Image. When the Apply Image dialog first appears, the Blending pop-up menu is set to Multiply (which generally makes the photo look way too dark). So, change the pop-up menu to Soft Light (our preferred Apply Image blend mode for making colors pop without making them too dark). Don't click OK yet.

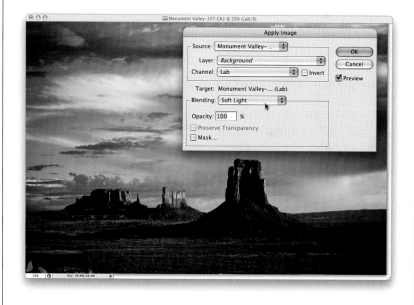

Step 12:

Once you've set the Blending pop-up menu to Soft Light, you now get to choose from three different "looks"—you simply choose which version looks best to you. You choose this from the Channel pop-up menu. The default look is the Lab channel, so choose "a" from the pop-up menu (as shown here), and then "b," and see which of those three you like the best. I'd say that the majority of the time I personally like the look of the Lab channel (which adds the most color and contrast). My second choice is usually the "a" channel, but in some photos, the "b" channel looks the best. There is no right answer—it's whichever of the three looks best to you (I liked "a" for this one, so let's go with "a"). Also, you can control the intensity of the effect by lowering the opacity. So go ahead and lower the Opacity amount here to 70% and then click OK.

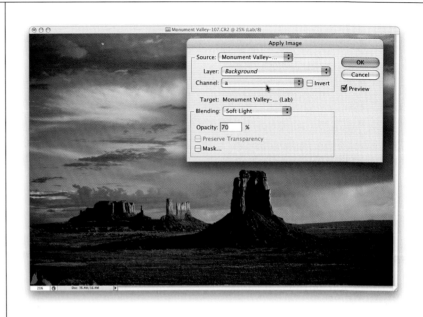

Step 13:

All the contrast we've added thus far has made the butte in the foreground look a little dark, so we'll need to open up those dark areas using a Shadow/Highlight adjustment (this is the third point of the 7-Point System). Start by pressing Command-J (PC: Ctrl-J) to duplicate the Background layer. Now, we could just open the Shadow/Highlight control and apply it directly to the image, but in a photo this colorful, it won't just open up those dark shadow areas, it will make the colors in those areas more saturated (and they're already pretty colorful). So to get around that, you can use another channels move. Go to the Channels panel (found under the Window menu) and click on the Lightness channel.

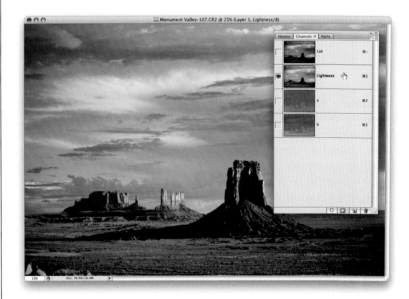

Step 14:
Now you're going to apply the Shadow/Highlight adjustment, but only to this Lightness channel. By doing this, you're only lightening the non-color areas (the luminosity in the photo, where all the detail is), which lets you open up the shadows without boosting the color in the shadows (this works really well). So now that you've clicked on the Lightness channel, go under the Image menu, under Adjustments, and choose Shadow/Highlight. The default settings generally open the shadow areas too much, and to me they look milky and artificial, so turn on the Show More Options checkbox (as shown here) to expand the dialog with additional options that will help us avoid that fake, milky look.

Step 15:
When the expanded Shadows/Highlights dialog appears, in the Shadows section, drag the Amount down to around 25%, increase the Tonal Width a little, and drag the Radius to between 250 and 300 pixels. These numbers are a good starting place, and using them opens the shadow areas, but avoids that fakey look. You could increase the Tonal Width to around 70 if you'd like, but that's pretty much as far as you want to take it. When it looks good to you, click OK.

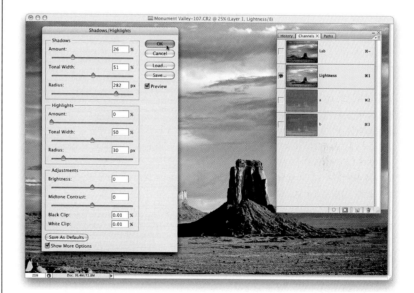

Step 16:
Go back under the Image menu, under Mode, and choose RGB Color. A dialog will appear asking you if you want to flatten your layers. Click Don't Flatten. Now, press-and-hold the Option (PC: Alt) key, and in the Layers panel, click on the Add Layer Mask icon at the bottom of the panel (as shown here), which adds a black mask over the layer where you just applied that Shadow/Highlight adjustment. So, think of that top layer as the "lighter" layer (even though it's hidden behind that black mask. Layer masks are part of the sixth point of the 7-Point System).

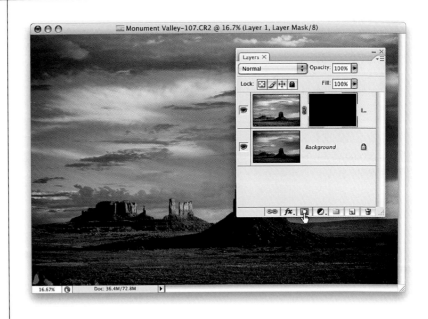

Step 17:
Now, we don't want to see the whole brighter layer, we just want the butte to be brighter (so basically, we only want to reveal the brighter layer right over the butte itself—we want to "paint with light"). To do that, press B to get the Brush tool, press X to set your Foreground color to white, and paint over the butte (as shown here) to reveal the lighter shadow areas and bring back some nice detail. This "painting with light" (painting brighter light onto our butte) is the fourth point of the 7-Point System. One more thing: it's pronounced "beaut" as in "she's a beauty," so stop giggling every time you say "butte."

Step 18:

If, after painting in the lighter version, you think it looks too light (or you think your adjustment is too obvious), just lower the opacity of this top layer until it looks more natural and blends right in (in this case, I lowered the Opacity setting to 76%). Now you can choose Flatten Image from the Layers panel's flyout menu to flatten these layers.

Step 19:

To make the sky more dramatic, we're going to use a quick layer blend mode trick (blend modes are also part of the sixth point of the 7-Point System). Start by pressing Command-J (PC: Ctrl-J) to duplicate the Background layer. Then change the layer blend mode to Multiply, which makes the sky (along with the entire photo) much darker. (*Note*: The other blend mode we use most often is Screen, which makes the photo much lighter.)

Step 20:

To make the top of the sky darker, while leaving the rest of the photo the same, we're going to, again, paint with light. Instead of using the Brush tool to reveal our darker layer, we're going to use the Gradient tool to smoothly blend from the normal image to the darker image up higher in the sky. To do that, Option-click (PC: Alt-click) on the Add Layer Mask icon at the bottom of the Layers panel to add a black mask over the darker Multiply layer. This hides it from view. Now, press G to grab the Gradient tool, choose the Black, White gradient, click just above the buttes in the background (I hear you snickering), and drag upward (as shown here). This gradually reveals the darker layer up towards the top of the image, making the top of the sky darker.

Step 21:

As always, if the result looks too dark (it does to me), just go to the Layers panel and lower the layer's opacity until it looks right to you (in this example, I lowered the Opacity to 79%). Now you can flatten the image, as we're ready to move on to sharpening—the seventh point of the 7-Point System. Our last step is always sharpening (well, that's the goal—to always sharpen as the last thing we do before we save the image, and we *always* sharpen). *Note:* We sharpen less if our final image will be viewed onscreen, in a slide show, or on the Web, and we sharpen more heavily if the image will become a print (at a photo lab or from your desktop inkjet or dye-sub printer).

Step 22:

In Lesson 1, I showed you how to make three different actions (Photoshop automations) that apply one-click sharpening (here, I clicked on Sharpen Medium in the Actions panel, then clicked the Play Selection icon). If you didn't create those actions, refer to Lesson 1 for the settings.

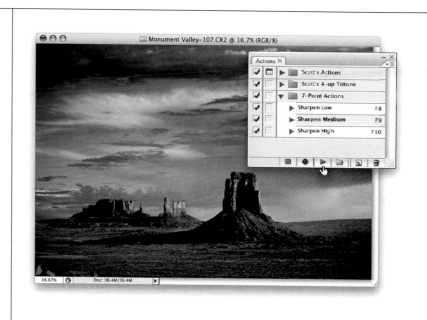

Before

After

1 Adobe Camera Raw Processing

Always start by processing your images in the Camera Raw plug-in (JPEG, TIFF, or RAW). Set your white balance first, then set your exposure, and once it's set, bring back any clipped highlights with the Recovery slider. Then use the Blacks slider to bring saturation to your colors in the shadow areas. Zoom in to 100% and add some clarity (as long as your subject isn't of a softer nature). If the photo needs more contrast, jump over to the Tone Curve panel, and use the Point Curve presets to add contrast. If you need to add sharpness, go to the Details panel. For landscape shots, increase the Detail amount. For portraits of women or children, increase the Masking amount instead. Now open the image in Photoshop.

2 Curves Adjustments

You probably won't have color problems at this point (if you balanced the color by setting the proper white balance while you were in Camera Raw), but you can use the presets at the top of the Curves dialog to add more contrast. Also, if you choose a Curves adjustment layer, you can use the Brush tool to paint over any areas that you don't want to have added contrast.

3 Shadow/Highlight

If your subject is backlit, or an area of important detail is in the shadows, switch to Lab color first, go to the Channels panel, and click on the Lightness channel. Then duplicate the Background layer, choose Convert for Smart Filters from the Filter menu, and choose Shadow/Highlight from the Image menu. Turn on the Show More Options checkbox, lower the Amount, increase the Threshold a little, and increase the Radius to between 250 and 300 to realistically open up the shadows. Switch back to RGB mode.

4 Painting with Light

If there are areas of your photo that you want darker or lighter, add a Curves adjustment layer, add a point to the center of the curve, and drag upward to make the photo brighter or down to make it darker. Then press Command-I (PC: Ctrl-I) to Invert the layer mask. Now paint in white to reveal the brighter (or darker) light right where you want it.

5 Channels Adjustments

To make the colors really pop, switch to Lab color again, then choose Apply Image from the Image menu. Set the Blending pop-up menu to Soft Light, then look at the Lab channel, the "a" channel, and the "b" channel, and choose the one that looks best. If the effect is too intense, lower the opacity only where you want it.

6 Layer Blend Modes & Layer Masks

To lighten your subject, or darken the sky, or a doorway, or generally control the tonal balance of the photo: duplicate the Background layer; choose the Screen blend mode to make your photo lighter, or Multiply to make it darker; then add a layer mask and paint in black to hide the effect, or Invert the mask (Command-I [PC: Ctrl-I]) to hide the effect, and paint in white to reveal the effect only where you want it.

7 Sharpening Techniques

Use the Unsharp Mask filter to sharpen your photo, then choose Fade Unsharp Mask immediately after, and change the Fade mode to Luminosity to avoid color problems. Try Amount: 85%, Radius: 1.0, and Threshold: 4 for a general medium amount of sharpening.

W

Y

Z

Really Right Stuff

your camera support experts

custom camera
L-plates – mount
in landscape
or portrait!

superior quick
release clamps

top-quality ballheads

...and the best
tripods available

from the ground up, Really Right Stuff® delivers gear you need

We design, build, aquire and sell the very best tripods, ballheads, quick-release clamps, and quick-release plates available anywhere. From the casual weekend shooter to the most demanding professional, discriminating photographers in over 80 countries around the globe rely on the experts at Really Right Stuff for all their camera support gear. Our quick-release system makes setup faster and easier, and better stability means better results. Call us now to receive a copy of our 68 page catalog, or visit us online at http://reallyrightstuff.com.

Available only at
Really Right Stuff
205 Higuera St
San Luis Obispo CA 93401 USA

http://reallyrightstuff.com
(805) 528-6321
or toll-free in US & Canada (888) 777-5557
Really Right Stuff® is a registered trademark of Really Right Stuff

Images courtesy of iStockphoto

ZOOM LENS FF-S 18-55mm 1:3.5-.6

85mm

It's not magic...
it's Photoshop!

Sometimes the perfect photo just happens...everything captured in its
exact detail. Other times there's Photoshop... Every day the
National Association of Photoshop Professionals shows thousands of
photographers how to turn ordinary photos into extraordinary art.

Join today and receive...

8 issues of *Photoshop User* magazine • unlimited access
to a massive collection of online tutorials • exclusive discounts and much more.
Plus, as a bonus, you'll get "The Best of *Photoshop User*: The Ninth Year" DVD
One-Year Membership $99* Use code NAPM-1UM for your gift.

NAPP National Association of Photoshop Professionals
The ultimate resource for Adobe® Photoshop® training, education, news, and more.

www.photoshopuser.com or call 800-738-8513